Vegetarian Barbecue

Vegetarian Barbecue

& Other Pleasures of the Harvest

BY PATTI A. BESS

LOWELL HOUSE

LOS ANGELES

CONTEMPORARY BOOKS

CHICAGO

Library of Congress Cataloging-in-Publication Data

Bess, Patti.
    Vegetarian barbecue : & other pleasures of the harvest / by
Patti Bess.
        p.   cm.
    Includes index.
    ISBN 1-56565-881-7
    1. Vegetarian cookery.   2. Barbecue cookery.   I. Title.
TX837.B484   1998
641.5'636—dc21   98-10710
                                                                    CIP

Copyright © 1998 by Patti A. Bess.
All rights reserved. No part of this work may be reproduced or transmit-
ted in any form or by any means, electronic or mechanical, including
photocopying or recording, or by any information storage or retrieval
system, except as may be expressly permitted by the 1976 Copyright Act
or in writing by the Publisher.

Requests for such permissions should be addressed to:
Lowell House
2020 Avenue of the Stars, Suite 300
Los Angeles, CA 90067

Lowell House books can be purchased at special discounts when ordered
in bulk for premiums and special sales.

Publisher: Jack Artenstein
Associate Publisher, Lowell House Adult: Bud Sperry
Managing Editor: Maria Magallanes
Text design: Laurie Young

Manufactured in the United States of America
10 9 8 7 6 5 4 3 2 1

THIS BOOK IS DEDICATED TO MY LIFELONG TEACHER,
PARAMAHANSA YOGANANDA.

Acknowledgments

I have to thank Bud Sperry, my publisher, for planting the seed idea of "vegetarian barbecue." I didn't know it at the time, but it is the cookbook I have wanted on my shelf for many years. Thanks also to Maria Magallanes who has been a great editor to work with.

I would also like to thank my husband, David Bess, who has been the official fire starter, taster, and most patient friend. And my children, Daniel and Theresa, for having the courage to taste so many new dishes with a minimum of wrinkled noses.

Thanks also go to Judi Stokes for all her encouragement; to Jean and Michael Baecker for being great tasters and for all Jean's comments and insights; to Susan and Steve Trombetta for their great organic produce; to Renee SchleyMay for day care; and to the many wonderful parents in the fifth-grade class at the Yuba River Charter School—they have been enthusiastic tasters and grill mates.

I'd especially like to thank Janet Miller for her computer expertise and my office mate, Jan Fishler, for her counsel, good humor, and consistent supply of treats. Thank you to Kristin Liljequist and Bruce Conklin as well as to my favorite neighbor Adelle Charlson (from San Jose, California) for letting me use some of her great recipes.

Thanks to Jay Hanson for lending me a variety of grills to play with and to Hasel Carter at Foxfire Wood Heat Systems in Grass Valley for her generous information. I'd also like to thank Dr. James Felton at the University of California Lawrence Livermore National Laboratories; the people at Spanish Table in Seattle, Washington, for their generosity and help in developing a meatless paella recipe; and the folks at the South Pine Street Cafe in Nevada City, California, for generously allowing me to use their nut burger recipe.

Contents

Introduction

Summer is my favorite time to cook. Having a garden full of fresh vegetables or shopping at the local farmers' market gives me a sense of opulence and abundance in life that no amount of wealth could ever duplicate.

As an addicted gardener, I have often dragged myself up to the kitchen, having stayed in the garden a little too long, and wished I had some new way of preparing the bowlful of freshly harvested produce. We all get into cooking ruts. But grilling is a new adventure and has rekindled my enthusiasm for food. Grilling is a simple and efficient cooking method that brings out the sweetness of vegetables and lets the food stand on its own merit.

People generally tend to eat less in hot summer weather, so it is a perfect time to put vegetables at the center of the dinner plate. Adopting a complete regimen of a meatless diet may not be the choice for everyone; but if you begin by including a few more meatless dishes on the grill every week, I know you will fall in love with the smoke-infused simplicity of the grilled dishes that follow.

Backyard barbecues or "wienie roasts," as my father still calls them, were always a highlight of summer when I was a child. They meant chasing cousins and friends around the neighborhood and playing hide-and-seek in the dark. In those days, except for an occasional trip to an outdoor movie, back-yard barbecues were the main summer attraction. Families and barbecues have changed a great deal since then—and that's an understatement!

The modern world is full of amusements and entertain-ments that pull each member of the family off into a different direction—diversions not particularly conducive to building strong families or communities. This book has been the stimulus for our family to entertain more. Now that our children are older, cookouts around the grill have become an economical entertainment that fits everyone's needs. We have discovered that laughing, playing games with the kids, providing a safe place for teenagers to hang out and work out their power struggles over a board game (rather than exhausting their parents with them) is very satisfying.

We have enjoyed getting to know many fascinating people, when previously we had time only for a passing hello. We have learned about their lives and enriched our own by discovering just how we all fit together to create a community—with no television to interfere with the simple pleasures of great food and good conversation.

Of course, the most important ingredient for a stimulating evening is good food around the grill and the camaraderie of preparing a meal together. Many times after these Friday Night Grilling Extravaganzas, I have fallen asleep with Dorothy's words on my lips, "There's no place like home! There's no place like home!"

1 ✳ CHAPTER

Meatless on the Grill

THE RHYTHM OF THE SEASONS IS INGRAINED IN MY DIETARY consciousness. I am hungry for potato salad the Monday after Easter, when I'm staring at baskets of hard-boiled eggs. I get out the stockpot for a bowl of hot soup on the first rainy day of October; and I long for a piece of my mother's Christmas candy as soon as the Thanksgiving leftovers are gone. Just about the time we spring forward into daylight savings time, my inner culinary clock says it's time to fire up the barbecue.

Barbecuing or grilling has been the sacrosanct domain of meat eaters since . . . well, I think the cavemen started the craze! But Americans have almost tunnel vision when it comes to grilling: Meat is what we cook. For many vegetarians, that wonderful smoky smell coming out of backyards everywhere has made us feel left out. As a vegetarian for many years, I often thought, "What would I do with a grill?"

Certain foods just seem to belong together—I call them taste marriages: raspberries and chocolate, peaches and cream, ketchup and mustard, grilling and meat. It is true that meats taste great cooked over the grill. But many other taste marriages beckon to be explored: polenta, eggplant, mushrooms, vegetables, and, yes, tofu. All these benefit from that intriguing smoky flavor that comes from grilling.

Grilling in America means good times, good friends, and great food. Welcome! The grill is heating up! If you are a vegetarian cook who longs for the taste of grilled food, or you thought grills were only for those with a stomach for blackened steaks and burgers, then come on in. With a small garden or a farmers' market close by and a grill on the deck, you are ready for a new adventure in cooking. Meatless grilling is limited only by the imagination of the cook.

If your family is not accustomed to meatless meals, I hope you will discover some side dishes full of grains, soy foods, and the captivating flavors of grilled vegetables—recipes that you can add to your grilling repertoire, eating less meat in the process. You might even discover that the dishes in this book are satisfying enough on a hot summer night so that meat is not the necessity you once thought it was. You won't know until you try!

Why Meatless?

For most of us, choosing a meatless lifestyle was a slow transition that evolved over a number of years. The important thing for most Americans is not that they eliminate meat altogether, but that they increase the grains and vegetables in their diet. Being totally vegetarian is probably not for everyone. I have learned (the hard way) that people are more willing to accept change when they play a part in making the choices. When my young children occasionally walk into the kitchen with long faces and say, "I hate being a vegetarian," then I surprise them with an evening of chicken on the grill. Once it's no longer a taboo, they really don't want it and, in fact, don't like it that much.

To our mothers, fathers, and grandparents, a meal was not complete unless it included a generous serving of meat. The United States Department of Agriculture's (USDA) four food groups—meat and fish, milk and eggs, fruits and vegetables, and bread and cereals—was the nutritional model that reigned for more than forty years.

Until the early 1980s, the majority of Americans clung to the conviction that they needed plenty of animal protein in order to have a healthy diet. Health and nutrition classes taught us what was mirrored on dinner tables throughout the country: Meat was the main course, and we were proud of it.

Since the turn of the century the United States has been the largest beef producer in the world. And it follows that we have one of the highest rates of meat consumption in the world. Meat, especially beef, has been a symbol of our affluence. It would be safe to say that meat eating is as much a part of our culture as are movies, baseball, and, of course, backyard barbecues. So telling the American public that meat need not be the central focus of their diet was akin to canceling Monday night football. But that's what the USDA and the Department of Health and Human Services did when they released the updated Dietary Guidelines for Americans and the Food Guide Pyramid in 1995.

The revised guidelines are the official blueprint for school lunches and other federal nutrition programs. For the first time, the USDA proposed moving grains, vegetables, and fruits to the center of the dinner plate, leaving meat, dairy products, and fats as minor players in the nutritional game plan and acknowledged the potential health benefits of a vegetarian diet.

A host of leading nutrition experts joined forces to assist in revamping the guidelines, which are updated every five years.

The proposal they submitted included more than one hundred scientific references showing that vegetarian diets can lead to dramatic reductions in heart disease, cancer, obesity, and other health risks.

How Much Protein Is Enough?

Nutritional science, like the field of technology, has seen astounding advances in the last twenty-five years. Today, few would think of buying a typewriter instead of a computer for their home office, but changing dietary habits instilled in early childhood is much more complex than learning to navigate the Internet. Many misconceptions about meat are still widely accepted as fact.

One such notion is that we need to eat meat to fulfill our daily requirements for protein. As any new vegetarian can attest, the first question asked by concerned friends is, inevitably, "How do you get enough protein?"

The traditional peasant diets of many cultures around the world have met protein needs by plant sources (grains, legumes, nuts, and soy) for thousands of years. People in these cultures do not develop the diseases of overnutrition that people in more developed countries do. In Asia the primary protein sources are rice and soy foods (with some fish). In South and Central America beans, corn, and rice are the main staples. Tabbouleh (cracked wheat), hummus (garbanzo beans), and pita bread are foundations of the diet in the Middle East (although meat is becoming more a part of the traditional diets of these countries as they become more Westernized).

Twenty-five years ago, our understanding of how much protein was necessary for an average-size adult male and female was 120 and 110 grams respectively. Today the RDAs (Recommended Daily Allowances) for protein for the same groups are 55 and 45 grams. "Aside from fat, if there is any one nutrient Americans consume in excess, it is protein. Most of us, including some vegetarians, get nearly twice the amount of protein we need," says the Harvard University *Women's Health Watch* newsletter.

Another myth that persists in American culture is the concept that plant sources of protein (grains, legumes, nuts, and soy) are inferior to animal foods and are "incomplete." In the 1970s and 1980s the "protein complementarity" concept was popularized by the landmark book *Diet for a Small Planet* by Frances Moore Lappe, which stated that to get enough protein from plant sources one would need to combine a variety of foods at one meal to make a "complete protein" capable of filling human nutritional needs. Studies in recent years have shown that this is unfounded. Suzanne Havala, M.S., R.D., the author of the position paper on vegetarianism for the American Dietetic Association, states, "As long as there are adequate calories from a variety of foods, protein takes care of itself. The balance of proteins over an entire day is of greater importance. No calculating of it is necessary to get adequate amounts."

Increasing the Ratio of Plant to Animal Foods

One thing is certain: The amount of meat most Americans consume is out of proportion to what is necessary, and decreasing the consumption of meat will, in the long run, extend not only the length of life but the quality as well. Meat is high in cholesterol and total fat, is devoid of fiber, and tends to displace plant foods on our menus. Modifying to a diet of lean meats, chicken, and low-fat dairy products still does not address the real problem with the American diet, which is increasing the ratio of plant to animal foods, says Havala. Plant foods are a rich source of vitamins, minerals, fiber, and phytochemicals, which have been shown to lower cholesterol levels and protect against heart disease, cancer, obesity, and diabetes.

Complete vegetarian diets are not necessary for everyone, nor would they be acceptable to most Americans. "There is a point at which meat would create very little harm if it were used as an ingredient of the meal, but not as the focal point of the entire diet as it tends to be in the U.S.," states Havala. The traditional dietary patterns of the Mediterranean peoples—plant-based, with dairy products, fish, meat, and poultry in small to moderate amounts—have been cited in many studies as a model that promotes low rates of chronic disease and high adult life expectancy.

Cooking more meatless meals on the grill is not about giving up meat. It's about expanding your repertoire to include new and exciting foods. There's no self-denial here—just deliciously healthy food choices that happen to be meatless. A dinner menu can consist of:

Polenta with Roasted Peppers and Fontina Cheese
Tomato Bruschettas
Grilled Portobello Mushroom and Asparagus Salad
Blueberry Peach Cobbler with Frozen Peach Yogurt

My hope for this book is that it will open new opportunities of grilling meatless meals—whether you're a vegetarian cook or you just want to experiment with using more vegetables and less meat.

Note: The symbol 🟊 denotes that the recipe is also vegan and contains no animal-based products including milk, butter, eggs, and lard. If a recipe uses Parmesan cheese as a garnish, it is marked "optional" and may be omitted to make it a vegan recipe. Parmesan cheese can be replaced with another choice like chives, nutritional yeast, or parsley for garnish. (If Parmesan cheese is an integral part of the recipe, though, it is not marked as vegan.)

Happy grilling and be well!

Grilling Basics

Ready, Set, Grill

From the trendiest restaurants to bookstore shelves full of cookbooks and the backyards of America, it's not hard to catch the grilling fever. The popularity of grilling and cooking outdoors has increased immensely in recent years.

Why? Grilling is fun because of its simplicity—not a lot of kitchen science is necessary. It is about taste, touch, and using your own judgment. There is something captivating and magnetizing about cooking over a fire, even if the fire is in a gas grill. Grilling also fits into our busy lives as it yields a maximum of flavor for a minimum of labor.

Choosing the Right Grill

There are two camps of people who love to barbecue: those who entertain or cook outdoors only occasionally, and the growing number of people who like to cook outdoors most of the summer season. When the weather is hot, lighting the kitchen stove becomes unthinkable so deciding what's for dinner starts with the question, "What can I cook on the grill?" Many people like the idea of moving the cooking outdoors to keep the house cooler and the kitchen less messy. Determining which of these situations applies to you and your family is an important part of knowing which type of grill best fits your needs.

As with any other appliance, ask yourself a few important questions before you make a purchase:

- Will I use the grill mainly for two people, for a larger family, or for entertaining larger groups of people?
- How much money am I willing to spend?
- Do I have a safe, convenient location to put a grill? Where will I store it in inclement weather?
- What accessories would I really use and like to have? (Many upgrades on grills are useful but some, like rotisseries, are unnecessary if you don't plan to cook meats.)

Types of Grills

You can buy a grill for as little as $29.95 for a smaller model. These will do almost as good a job grilling as the large models, but smaller models are not large enough to grill four vegeburgers or a few green peppers at a time. You can also spend up to $5,000 for a built-in brick grill and oven that can do everything (except balance the checkbook) and look like a million bucks in the backyard.

No matter what type of grill you choose, read the manufacturer's instructions. Success with grilling begins with knowing your particular grill and how to use it.

Charcoal grills To many people, grilling just isn't grilling unless they are cooking over a real fire. I must agree that this is an ideal cooking situation. It feels more authentic. The flavor of the food is most enhanced by a wood (or briquette) fire. If you are one of those people, a charcoal kettle grill is the best choice.

Charcoal grills are by far the least expensive investment. A covered grill as opposed to an open brazier-type grill will give you more flexibility for vegetarian grilling and is easier to regulate the heat.

Charcoal grills do have a few drawbacks: If you want to cook in the backyard on a regular basis, the charcoal grill is probably not the best choice. Coals need about 30 minutes to develop a fire of the right temperature and are not always easy to light. Cleanup for charcoal grills can be very messy, and upkeep is also more difficult.

Regulating heat on a charcoal grill can also be somewhat tricky. To increase the heat for a charcoal grill, tap the coals to remove the white ash and push them closer together. Lower the heat by spreading the coals apart. One great feature of some higher-end charcoal grills is a grate that can be raised or lowered to control the temperature conveniently. Spits are another feature of higher-end charcoal grills. These enhance the cooking of meats but are of little use to someone who plans to grill meatless dishes. A feature that provides an easy method for cleaning out the coals is well worth the extra cost. Larger kettle-type grills also have a more convenient cooking grate that is hinged on two sides so that additional coals may be added to the fire without having to take the food off the grill.

A kettle grill that is 21 to 24 inches should be a minimum size for the recipes in this book. It takes more surface space to cook a variety of vegetarian foods as opposed to putting a few pieces of meat on the grill. Also, many of the recipes in this book use indirect heat which takes at least 21 inches of grill space.

Gas grills Many people, however, don't have the time to build a fire and wait for the coals to burn down. This is one of the reasons why gas grills make up about 75 percent of the grills sold in America today. Gas grills are a compromise to some people, but if you plan to make grilling your primary cooking method during the summer, you will quickly discover why gas grills are indeed the easiest and most convenient to use on a regular basis.

Better quality gas grills offer much more versatility and reliability in temperature control. Gas grills are available with one to four burners. Some even have a small burner on the side for warming sauce or boiling pasta. Again, many features of gas grills are for the purpose of cooking meats so ask questions when shopping. Sturdy side shelves are also a helpful benefit.

Electric grills These seem to be getting better every year, but for the most part, electric grills don't heat to the temperatures needed for grilling.

Pellet grills These have been on the market for approximately five years now. They cook with small wood pellets and have the advantage of giving that wood flavor without having to build a fire with briquettes. They heat up fairly quickly and are about equal in their costs of heating. They aren't particularly good for vegetarian grillers but great for those who cook and/or smoke a lot of meats.

Two Ways to Barbecue

Many people think to use their grill for only one cooking function: grilling. Grills can also be used for slow roasting and baking, making them a much more versatile appliance for vegetarian grillers.

Direct heat—Grilling On a kettle grill this is done by opening the bottom dampers (if the barbecue has them) and removing the lid. Spread the briquettes on the fire grate in a solid layer that is 1 to 2 inches larger than the area you intend to use for food. Set the grill at the recommended height and brush with vegetable oil before placing food on it. To maintain even heat, scatter ten new briquettes over the bed every 30 minutes.

To create direct heat for grilling on a gas grill, merely preheat the grill to the desired temperature.

Indirect heat—Roasting or baking This is best done on a kettle grill that is at least 21 to 24 inches in diameter. (It doesn't work well on small portable grills.) Start with coals that are cooled to a medium intensity. You can grill foods that need a higher temperature first. With a long-handled spatula, move the coals over to one side of the grill and place the dish to be baked on the opposite side. Cover and roast.

Gas grills will provide an indirect source of heat even more easily. If you have more than two burners on your gas grill, heat the outside burners and place the dish on the middle unheated burner; close the lid. If you have only two burners, preheat both to medium, turn one off, and place the bread or casserole on that burner; close the lid. For gas grills with two burners, check the dish at least halfway through the cooking and turn it to ensure even heating. Many gas grills also have a warming rack where a small dish or bread could be placed for baking. Some gas grills tend to have hot spots so, again, get to know your particular grill.

Fuel for the Fire

Charcoal briquettes are the most commonly used fuel. They are widely available and are a good choice, but look for regular briquettes. Instant-lighting charcoal briquettes are impregnated with a chemical starter and light very easily, but they leave a lingering chemical smell and are not environmentally safe.

Organic charcoal briquettes made without fillers and out of nutshells instead of wood products are available at many natural-food stores. They are more expensive but seem to burn longer and hotter.

Natural or propane gas Gas grills may use either one of these.

Ceramic briquettes, volcanic lava rocks, metal bars Juices drip onto ceramic briquettes, volcanic lava rocks, or metal bars above the burner, causing smoke to rise and flavor the food.

Lump charcoal burns about twice as hot as charcoal briquettes and smells cleaner. It is becoming more available but is still sometimes difficult to locate. It also has small pockets of moisture in the lumps, which cause small pops and can throw sparks. Though lump charcoal costs more than regular briquettes, you'll need only half as much for a fire of similar heat intensity.

Flavorful wood chips make a more convenient and satisfactory grill fuel than wood itself; wood is best only for imparting a smoky flavor. Hardwoods such as alder, oak, mesquite, and hickory impart the most taste to grilled foods. Vegetables tend to taste best grilled over mesquite. Maple and some fruit tree woods are also commonly used. Woods such as pine or cedar should not be used, as they leave a sticky resin on food. Varieties of wood chips are available at most hardware and grocery stores.

If you have access to wood on your own property, cut it into small chips for use. It must be well dried but not rotted. The best smoky fragrance comes from wood chips soaked in water for about 30 minutes before being added in small amounts to the coals of a kettle grill. This can be done on a gas grill by placing the wood chips under the grill in a heavy-duty foil container in which holes have been punched, or wrapping the chips in aluminum foil, to add a smoky flavor.

If you are cooking food that will only stay on the grill for less than 5 minutes, using flavorful woods for smoke doesn't make a big flavor difference.

Starting the Fire

Preparing a fire in an electric or gas grill is as simple as turning on a switch. Every grill is different. Follow the manufacturer's directions for preheating.

Most electric grills will heat up in 3 to 10 minutes. Gas grills may take as long as 15 minutes.

Building a fire in a kettle grill is a longer process, but it is a ritual that many people (especially those of the male gender) savor. Avoid gasoline, kerosene, or lighter fluid to start the fire. Gasoline and kerosene are dangerous as well as being hazardous to your health. They impart an unpleasant taste to grilled foods. Lighter fluid is a chemical called naphthalene, an air pollutant and possible carcinogen.

Perhaps the best invention for lighting fires that has come along recently is the metal chimney. It is an inexpensive, straight sided metal cylinder. To light a fire in it you merely set the chimney on the fire grate and crumple up newspaper in the bottom section. Pour charcoal into the top section and light the newspaper with a match. In about 20 minutes the underside of the top coals should be hot and ready to use. Holding onto the wooden handle, you turn the coals out onto the grill and spread them out for use.

Safe, clean, solid synthetic fire starters are also widely available. They are a waxy, corklike substance sold under various commercial names and usually found where wood stoves or barbecues are sold. They cost little to use. Simply fill the base of the grill with as many briquettes as desired. Tear the fire starter into small pieces and scatter it among the coals. (Make sure the pieces are large enough so that they don't fall through the holes in the bottom of your grill.) Light two or three of them and you'll have a good fire going in minutes.

Of course, there is also the old-fashioned way of arranging a few dry twigs and small branches over a loose pile of crumpled newspaper, covering it with a pyramid of charcoal, and lighting the paper. This method, however, is not appropriate for most locations as stray bits of burning paper may blow loose and set fire to something nearby.

Care of the Grill

Many grills in the backyards of America rust out before they wear out. To protect your investment, buy a well-fitted plastic cover for your grill or be sure to have a protected place to store it when inclement weather comes.

Brush the grill rack with oil each time you use it to lessen the chance of food sticking. A 1-inch paintbrush will work well for this purpose. To prevent oil from turning rancid throw the paintbrush in the dishwasher after each use or wash it in warm water. If you use a nonstick vegetable cooking spray, remember to spray the rack before the grill is heated.

To clean a gas grill and burn off the residual food, heat the barbecue for a short time when food has been removed. Brush the rack with a stiff wire brush to loosen charred bits of food. If necessary, soak the grill in TSP, a cleaning powder available in hardware stores. Never use commercial oven cleaners, as they contain toxic substances that can be subsequently transferred to food. Once a season remove the lava rocks and clean the interior of the gas grill to improve its efficiency.

The ashes in a kettle grill must be removed after each use. Cleaning the grill as described above for gas grills is also necessary. Kettle grills need protection from damp weather to prevent rust.

Fire Safety

With a little common sense and a healthy amount of caution, grilling is a safe and fun activity. Follow these guidelines:

- Do not grill indoors unless a unit is specifically designed for it.
- Make sure the site is clear of flammable objects such as overhanging branches or leaves and brush around the base of the grill. If you must grill on a wood deck, either wet the area or place the grill on a brick or metal surface such as a flat piece of sheet metal.
- Have water or baking soda nearby to extinguish flames in an emergency.
- Avoid charcoal fires on windy days.
- Lift a grill cover away from your face to avoid burns from smoke or steam.
- Loose-fitting clothing that could impede movement or long flowing sleeves can be dangerous.
- Never attempt to move a hot grill.
- Use long-handled cooking tools and wear protective mitts or use heavy-duty pot holders when touching any of the grill parts or removing dishes from the fire.

Is Grilling Safe?

Many of us think that it's those little black briquettes that may be hazardous to our health, but scientists at Lawrence Livermore Laboratory at the University of California, Berkeley, have studied both gas and briquette fires and found them about equal in their potentially dangerous emissions.

The primary problem with carcinogens lies in the grilling of meats—more specifically, the charring of them. When meats are cooked over 300 degrees Fahrenheit, potent carcinogens called heterocyclic aromatic amines, or HAAs, are formed.

They are strong mutagens that cause cancer in laboratory animals. A second carcinogen is formed from barbecue smoke. When fat drips onto coals, polyaromatic hydrocarbons are produced. They rise back up and affect the food. Conclusive animal studies have convinced scientists that this is an area they need to continue to study. These two carcinogens are not formed in vegetable-based foods or vegetable fats as far as they know.

Scientists at Lawrence Livermore Labs also took a look at some of the artificial meat products and various grains and were surprised to find that they had a high degree of HAAs as well, but only about one one-hundredth as strong as in muscle meats.

So what can one do to minimize the health risks of cooking over a grill? First of all, eating less meat and including more vegetables is an excellent step. Choosing lean cuts of meat is also helpful. For vegetarians, minimize the amount of fat in marinades that can drip down on coals. Second, don't overcook foods. Much of the carcinogenicity increases as foods are cooked at higher temperatures for longer periods of time. An overcooked pizza tested at the Lawrence Livermore Labs had a tremendously high rate of carcinogenicity. The moral of the story: Stay near your grill and cook foods only as long as necessary.

How Hot Is the Fire?

Hot A fire in the grill is considered hot if you can hold your hand 6 inches above the grill for only 2 to 3 seconds, and coals are barely covered with ash.

Medium A fire is considered medium if you can hold your hand 6 inches above the grill for 4 to 5 seconds. Coals glow red through a layer of gray ash.

Low The fire is at a low temperature if you can hold your hand 6 inches above the grill for at least 6 to 7 seconds. Coals are covered with a thick layer of ash.

Useful Tools and Accessories

Basting brushes These are needed for brushing the grill rack with oil so that food will not stick as well as for brushing foods with marinades or olive oil during grilling. A good-quality brush at least 1½ inches wide is essential. A natural bristle paintbrush works well. It's not worth buying a bargain brush because the bristles will come out onto the food. Ideally, two brushes are best—one for oiling the grill and one for brushing marinades onto food.

Cleaning brush Use a stiff wire brush for cleaning the grill rack and for removing heavily burned-on food bits.

Grill screen This is especially useful for grilling small pieces of food that might fall through the wider grate of the grill, or for more delicate foods such as tofu, onion rings, and vege-burgers. There are also round pizza warming screens available, which could be used for grilling delicate foods as well as pizza. I find this has been my best investment as I can use it for two or three purposes: putting vegetable burgers on the grill and as a tray for grilling thin slices of bread.

Grill basket This allows you to grill larger amounts of small items that may be difficult to turn such as tofu, slices of squash, peppers, burgers, and soy hot dogs, which tend to fall apart more easily than meat-based hot dogs. Adjustable grill baskets are available and have the added advantage of accommodating a variety of foods of different heights.

Heavy aluminum foil When aluminum foil is needed, lighter-weight foils can easily break and make a mess. Use a minimum of three layers if using lighter-weight aluminum foil.

Non-metallic marinade dish Use a glass cake pan or a shallow wide ceramic dish to marinate foods.

Oven mitts Extra-long cuffs give more protection to arms when working with a charcoal kettle grill.

Rice cooker This is an indispensable piece of equipment for families who prepare rice on a regular basis. It automatically cooks all types of rice without burning or scorching.

Skewers Look for square or twisted metal skewers. These hold food in place better so that when you turn the food it doesn't twist. Bamboo skewers are also available at most cooking or barbecue stores and come in a variety of lengths. They are relatively inexpensive unless you make kabobs often; they only last for one or two uses. They must be soaked in water for 30 minutes before using so that they do not burn when exposed to the grill's high heat.

Spatula A long-handled, stainless steel spatula with a wide blade and an angled neck works best. On smaller gas grills the long handle can be cumbersome. An extra-long-handled spatula is helpful for moving hot coals in a kettle grill.

Tongs Long-handled tongs with smooth tips will turn food without tearing it. Do not use forks as they will pierce foods and allow juices to escape.

Staples for Grilling

Creative summer dinners can happen more easily if you keep some important staples on hand. (Wine for cooking and for sipping is also most helpful.)

Bulgur is cracked, partially cooked wheat. It is available in bulk (usually the least expensive form) at most natural-food stores. In supermarkets it is found in packages. Bulgur is nutritious, an important source of fiber, and cooks in less than 5 minutes.

Cheeses At one time we all piled our plates with ooey-gooey cheese. To keep vegetarian dishes low in fat, cheese can be used in small amounts for flavoring. When reducing the amount of cheese in a recipe, it is helpful to increase other strong flavor-enhancing foods such as herbs, garlic, lemon juice, red wine, olives, or miso.

Couscous is a finely cracked pasta. The least expensive way to buy it is in bulk in natural-food stores. It is sold packaged in supermarkets. It cooks in 3 to 4 minutes.

French bread is essential for a variety of uses and pleasures.

Fresh herbs are a flavor-enhancing asset to any cook. Most require little attention once planted and can be grown on a small mound outside the kitchen door or in barrels on a deck. They are becoming more available in supermarkets (though not always very fresh). Dried herbs are an acceptable alternative and more convenient.

Garlic Minced, chopped, roasted, or raw, garlic is the foundation of great cooking (and those that use it extensively are never bothered by colds or vampires!).

Marinades are used extensively to give grilled foods great flavor. The time needed for soaking depends on the size of the cut-up food. Tofu is best drained and marinated for a minimum of 12 hours.

Olive oil is essential for grilling. Both a regular, good-quality olive oil and a bottle of extra-virgin oil are helpful to have on hand. Use the extra-virgin when you need the most flavor for the least amount of fat. Cooking extra-virgin oil can diminish its flavor.

Olives A variety of olives are available today. They are great for adding a boost of flavor without a lot of fat. Kalamata olives, a Greek uncured olive with a strong flavor, are used often in combination with feta cheese.

Parmesan cheese It's helpful to have both dried and fresh Parmesan on hand, as the two types function very differently. Take your calculator to the store as you shop in the deli—you will discover that fresh Parmesan may cost less than the salty packaged kinds that have additives.

Pasta Essential as a side dish or topped with grilled vegetables.

Pine nuts Also called pinions, these flavorful nuts taste delicious when slightly roasted. They are used in pesto and other basil dishes.

Rice Most people think rice is just rice, but various rices will function better in different dishes. A long-grain rice is best used when distinct, separate kernels are desired. A short-grain rice is used when it is more desirable for the rice to hold together as in sushi or vegetable burgers. Arborio rice is a medium-grain rice that has the ability to absorb a great deal of moisture. It is used in risottos or paellas (a special Spanish rice is available also). Basmati is a rice that was originally grown in India; good basmati-type rice is now grown in the United States, sold under different names. Basmati is mildly fragrant with a flavor similar to popcorn.

White milled rice has been fortified with some vitamins and minerals, but it is still lacking in fiber, which most Americans are desperately in need of—especially those who eat predominantly meat diets. Brown rice is an unhulled rice that has the same amount of protein as white rice, but almost twice the amount of fiber. It is also higher in vitamins and minerals that are not added to white rice. It is very easy to adjust to the nuttier flavor of brown rice.

Vinegars Many types are called for in this book. Each has a distinct flavor appropriate for a particular dish. White and red wine vinegars are the most common. Rice wine vinegar is slightly sweeter. Sherry wine vinaigrette and flavored vinegars give salads a subtle touch. Balsamic vinegar is particularly good for marinades and sauces when grilling because it is particularly mellow and slightly sweet.

3 ✳ CHAPTER

Polenta, Tofu, Pasta, Grains, and Other Hearty Main Dishes

ONE OF THE THINGS I LOVE MOST ABOUT VEGETARIAN cooking and dining is the unlimited ways a meal can be assembled—especially in summer when people want to eat lighter foods. The main focus may be a hearty bruschetta with a bowl of gazpacho or a meal that is built around a delicious couscous salad. The repertoire of foods in a vegetarian meal is expansive. For people who are just beginning to experiment with meatless meals, there may be a sense that something central to the meal is missing, but the recipes that follow all contain good protein sources to replace meat.

Hearty main dishes for a meatless meal might focus on polenta, tofu, rice, potatoes, or pasta. Beans, though not cooked often on a grill, are included in chapter 4. Some of the main dish ideas included in this chapter may be less appropriate for the grill, but I include them to provide a perspective of what can be eaten as protein sources.

Polenta

Polenta is an Italian staple. Polenta celebrations, which traditionally commemorated the overcoming of famine or other adversities, are still held in Italy today.

Polenta can be as satisfying to make as it is to eat. There is a certain sensuous pleasure in stirring the golden mixture. You'll develop your own sense of feeling it take shape under the spoon and will savor the luscious corn smell released as it cooks. In hot summer weather I make it early in the morning, then it's ready to cut and grill for dinner later that day. Polenta takes to the grill like berries take to cream.

Making polenta is a good investment of my time since I get two, possibly three, great meals out of one recipe. You can store polenta in the refrigerator for up to five days or freeze it for later use.

Some people shy away from making polenta because they think it involves hours of preparation. Polenta actually takes 25 minutes to cook from start to finish. Instant polenta that comes in a tube can be purchased in most stores. It's a convenient way of using polenta in small amounts. If you don't have time to make your own, it's an acceptable alternative.

Basic Polenta

6½ cups water
1 teaspoon salt
2 cups polenta

1 tablespoon butter
or margarine
¼ cup grated Parmesan cheese
(optional)

1. Bring water to a boil in a large stockpot. Add salt.
2. Sprinkle in polenta gradually, stirring constantly with a wooden spoon. When all of the polenta has been added, reduce heat to low. Cook and stir until polenta begins to thicken and pull away from the sides of the pan, about 20 minutes. Add butter and Parmesan cheese the last 2 to 3 minutes of cooking.
3. Remove from heat. Spread polenta on a baking sheet and cut into squares, or spread it into two 9-inch pie pans and cut into wedges. The method depends on how you like to serve it. You can also use cookie cutters to make a variety of shapes or circles of polenta. If you plan to grill it, a slice 1 to 1½ inches thick is most manageable on the grill.

MAKES APPROXIMATELY 18 SERVINGS.

Serving Suggestions: Spread a 9-inch circle of polenta on a cookie sheet. Cut out a small area from the center. Fill this space with Caponata and place on the grill to warm through (see page 196).

Polenta with Roasted Peppers and Fontina Cheese

This easy-to-prepare dish consists of the best of summer—peppers, polenta, and tomatoes.

3 large bell peppers (a mix of colors)	Nonstick vegetable cooking spray
1 14.5-ounce can stewed tomatoes, undrained and chopped	½ recipe for Basic Polenta (page 25) or 10 squares of cooked polenta
3 tablespoons chopped fresh basil	1½ cups (6 ounces) shredded fontina cheese

1. Preheat a gas grill to medium or build a fire in a kettle grill.
2. Cut peppers in half lengthwise; discard seeds and membranes. Place pepper halves on the heated grill for 8 to 10 minutes, turning them often until evenly charred. Place peppers in a plastic bag and close bag. Let stand 10 minutes to cool and finish steaming in the bag. When cool enough to handle, peel the blackened skin from the peppers. Cut peppers into strips and set aside.
3. Pour the can of tomatoes into a large bowl and mash with a potato masher. Add the pepper strips and chopped basil.
4. Spread half the tomato/pepper sauce in the bottom of a 9-by-13-inch baking dish sprayed with cooking spray. (Use a metal cake pan or purchase a disposable aluminum foil baking pan for the grill.) Arrange slices of polenta over the sauce; spread remaining pepper sauce over polenta. Sprinkle with cheese and cover with aluminum foil.

5. For a gas grill with two burners, set one burner at medium and place the baking dish on the other burner. For a kettle grill, move the medium-hot coals to one side of the kettle and place the baking dish on the opposite side. Cover grill and roast for about 15 to 20 minutes or until warmed through. This dish can also be baked in the oven at 350 degrees for 15 to 20 minutes.

MAKES 6 TO 8 SERVINGS.

Polenta Casserole
with Summer Squash
and Sweet Peppers

2 teaspoons olive oil

2 teaspoons butter

1 small onion, coarsely chopped

1 red bell pepper (discard seeds and membrane), cut into ½-inch dice

2 small red-skinned new potatoes, cut into ½-inch dice

3 cloves garlic, minced

2 medium-size yellow squash, cut into ¾-inch dice

½ cup polenta

¼ cup all-purpose flour or whole-wheat pastry flour

¼ cup freshly grated Parmesan cheese

1 tablespoon fresh thyme leaves

1 teaspoon salt

¾ teaspoon freshly ground black pepper

1 cup milk

1 large egg plus 1 egg white

6 tablespoons grated Gruyère cheese (about 2 ounces)

1. Build a fire in a kettle grill or preheat one burner of a gas grill to medium. Generously rub a 9-inch-square baking dish with olive oil.
2. In a large, heavy skillet, melt the butter and 2 teaspoons olive oil over moderately high heat. Add the onion, bell pepper, and potatoes and cook, stirring, for 3 to 5 minutes. Stir in the garlic and cook until the vegetables are partially softened but not browned, about 2 minutes. Add the squash; cook, stirring, until almost tender, about 4 minutes. Set aside.
3. In a large bowl, toss together the polenta, flour, Parmesan, thyme, salt, and pepper. In a separate bowl, whisk together the milk and eggs, then

whisk them into the polenta mixture until combined. Stir the vegetables into the loose batter and spread it in the prepared baking dish. (The mixture will be fairly liquid.)

4. Cover dish with aluminum foil and place over indirect heat on a medium-hot grill or on the middle shelf of a 350-degree oven for 25 to 30 minutes, or until firm. Remove the aluminum foil for the last 15 minutes on the grill. Sprinkle the Gruyère on top for the last 7 minutes, or until golden around the edges. Cut into squares and serve hot or at room temperature.

MAKES 6 TO 8 SERVINGS.

Grilled Polenta
with Mushrooms

The mushroom sauce in this recipe is even more delectable if you use a combination of portobello, shiitake, and button mushrooms.

½ recipe for Basic Polenta (page 25), cut in squares or wedges

1 tablespoon extra-virgin olive oil

2 tablespoons butter

1 medium-size onion, finely chopped

1 pound fresh mushrooms, sliced

3 cloves garlic, minced

3 tablespoons soy sauce

3 tablespoons dry sherry

¼ cup well-flavored vegetable broth, cool

1 teaspoon cornstarch

½ teaspoon salt

Freshly ground black pepper

¼ cup freshly grated Parmesan cheese

1. Preheat a gas grill to medium-high or build a fire in a kettle grill.
2. Brush polenta slices with olive oil; set aside.
3. In a large skillet, sauté the onion in butter. Add the mushrooms and garlic; sauté for 4 to 5 additional minutes. Add the soy sauce and sherry and turn heat to low. Stir cornstarch into the cool vegetable stock. Add the stock to the mushrooms and bring to a boil until thickened—about 2 to 3 minutes. Season with salt and pepper.
4. Grill polenta, turning only once, until grill lines form and polenta has a slightly crispy crust—about 4 minutes on each side. Top each slice with a generous spoonful of the mushroom sauce and a pinch of Parmesan cheese. Serve this dish with freshly warmed bread or bruschetta and a tossed green salad or grilled vegetables.

MAKES 6 TO 8 SERVINGS.

Variation: Top with a tomato sauce and freshly grated Parmesan cheese.

Tofu

Degraded, ridiculed, and underrated, tofu is in dire need of an image makeover. For many people, their first experiences of this soy product were so tasteless and bland, they turned away disgusted and unimpressed. Even though dietitians are singing the praises of eating more soy foods these days, many people look nervously toward the door when tofu is mentioned.

I always tell people that tofu's greatest strength is its greatest weakness. Its greatest strength is that it will absorb the flavors around it. Its greatest weakness is that it has no desirable flavor of its own. As a cooking ingredient, it has tremendous potential and takes to the grill wonderfully.

Firm or extra-firm tofu will hold together better than tofu labeled "regular" or "soft" and will work best for the grilling recipes in this book. Always drain the tofu so that its water content will not dilute the flavor of the sauce and it can absorb marinades more easily.

One method for draining is to set the tofu square on a bread board or baking sheet and raise one end, with the lower end pointed toward the sink. Cover the tofu with plastic wrap or another tray and place a cookbook or anything heavy on top. I have also put tofu in a colander, topped with plastic wrap, and placed a vase or large can on top of it. Allow tofu to drain at least 30 minutes.

In most instances, tofu needs a minimum of 12 hours to absorb the flavors of a marinade. That takes no extra time at all—just planning ahead. Tofu is still usable if such a long marinade is not possible, but it will not be as flavorful.

❈ Marinated Tofu

1 pound package firm
or extra-firm tofu

Sesame Marinade (page 142) or
Teriyaki Marinade (page 143)

1. Rinse and drain tofu as described above.
2. Unless it is already cut that way, slice tofu into slabs 1 inch thick. Pour
   marinade into a shallow, wide dish (glass or ceramic is best). Arrange
   tofu in a single layer, cover, and refrigerate. For best tofu flavor, allow it
   to marinate at least 24 hours. Tofu marinated up to 3 days tastes even
   better. Use for Teriyaki Tofu Steaks or Burgers (page 66).

Barbecue Tofu

1 pound package firm or extra-firm tofu	1 to 1½ cups Barbecue Sauce (page 150)

1. Rinse and drain tofu as described on page 31.
2. Pour ½ cup of the Barbecue Sauce in the bottom of a wide, shallow baking or cake pan (glass or ceramic is best). Cut tofu into slices ½ inch thick. Add tofu to the baking dish and pour ½ to ¾ cup more Barbecue Sauce over it. Cover and refrigerate overnight or at least for 2 hours. Turn the tofu occasionally during that time.
3. Build a fire in a kettle grill or preheat a gas grill.
4. Place tofu in a grilling basket or use a pizza warming pan. Grill until heated through, basting with the additional Barbecue Sauce.

MAKES 4 SERVINGS.

❋ Tofu-Stuffed Peppers on the Grill

I used to make this dish years ago with hamburger. Here I use tofu. The texture of the tofu will be more crumbly and meatlike if you freeze it first, then thaw and drain well.

4 large green peppers	½ to ¾ teaspoon salt
1 large onion, diced	1 teaspoon fresh oregano
3 cloves garlic, chopped or minced	1 tablespoon soy sauce
12 ounces tofu, crumbled	1 14.5-ounce can stewed tomatoes
2 tablespoons olive oil	1 cup cooked brown rice
8 ounces mushrooms, washed and sliced	½ cup water
4 Roma tomatoes	Freshly ground black pepper
1 teaspoon minced fresh marjoram	Garnish: Parmesan cheese or sour cream (optional)

1. Preheat a gas grill to medium-high or build a fire in a kettle grill.
2. When the frozen tofu has thawed completely, drain as described above for at least 30 minutes.
3. With a small paring knife, cut off the tops of the green peppers and scoop out all seeds and inner membrane. Place whole peppers on the grill for about 5 minutes total, turning them every 2 minutes until they are lightly charred but not overly softened. Set aside to cool.
4. In a large skillet on the stove or on the (gas) grill, sauté the onion, garlic, and tofu in olive oil, about 4 to 5 minutes. Add the mushrooms; 3 Roma

tomatoes, diced; marjoram, salt, and oregano. Sauté for another 3 to 5 minutes. Add the soy sauce, stewed tomatoes, and the rice. Stir to mix; remove from heat.

5. Fill each pepper with this mixture, pushing down gently with a spoon to make more space for the stuffing. Quarter one Roma tomato and wedge one quarter into the top of each pepper. Place the peppers in a 2-quart baking dish and pour the remaining tomato mixture around the peppers. Add the water and black pepper; cover with aluminum foil.

6. Place on the grill and cook over indirect heat (see directions in chapter 2, page 11) for 20 to 25 minutes or until peppers feel fork-tender but not mushy. Spoon the extra sauce over the peppers and garnish with a dollop of sour cream or Parmesan cheese.

MAKES 4 SERVINGS, OR 8 AS A SIDE DISH.

Frittatas

Frittatas, a sort of unfolded omelet, are a familiar part of Italian cuisine. They are somewhat lower in fat than quiche because they lack a crust. Frittatas can easily be made on the grill. Turning the pan will help them to cook evenly.

Summer Garden Frittata

If you use a kettle grill for this recipe, you may want to grill other foods first. Then when the grill has cooled to a medium temperature, prepare it for indirect heating as described in chapter 2, page 11.

4 eggs plus 2 egg whites
¼ teaspoon white pepper
¾ cup freshly grated Parmesan cheese
1 tablespoon extra-virgin olive oil
1 small onion, finely chopped
2 cloves garlic, minced

2 small zucchini or yellow crookneck squash, grated
8 to 10 large basil leaves, finely chopped
1 medium-size tomato, seeded and chopped
Nonstick vegetable cooking spray or 2 teaspoons vegetable oil

1. Preheat one burner of a gas grill or build a fire in a kettle grill and prepare for indirect heat.
2. Beat eggs, egg whites, pepper, and Parmesan together in a small bowl and set aside.
3. Heat oil in a wide frying pan over medium-high heat. Add onion; sauté 3 to 4 minutes, until onion is translucent. Add garlic, squash, basil, and tomato; continue to sauté for an additional 2 minutes until vegetables are crisp-tender. Add vegetables to the egg mixture.
4. Spray a 9-inch round deep-dish pie pan with nonstick vegetable spray or rub with oil. Pour mixture into prepared pan. Place on the grill for 25 to 30 minutes or until eggs are set in the center, turning once to ensure even heat. (The frittata can also be baked in a 350-degree oven for 30 minutes.)
5. Remove pan from the grill. Allow to cool slightly before cutting frittata. Serve hot or at room temperature.

MAKES 6 TO 8 SERVINGS.

Frittata
with Garden Greens

Try this frittata with a combination of two different greens. It has sensational flavor and is low in fat. Cut into slices as an appetizer or entrée.

1 tablespoon olive oil	⅛ teaspoon freshly ground
½ small red onion, finely	black pepper
chopped	¼ teaspoon nutmeg
2 cloves garlic, minced	½ teaspoon crumbled dry basil
4 cups garden greens, such as	½ cup low-fat cottage cheese
chard, kale, escarole,	½ cup grated Parmesan cheese
or spinach, washed and	Nonstick vegetable cooking
finely chopped	spray or vegetable oil
4 eggs plus 2 egg whites	

1. Preheat one burner of a gas grill to medium or build a fire in a kettle grill.
2. Heat olive oil in a wide frying pan over medium-high heat. Add the onion and garlic and sauté for 2 to 3 minutes, until onion is translucent. Add the chopped greens, cover, and steam just until greens have wilted—about 2 minutes. Set aside to cool.
3. Beat eggs and egg whites lightly with pepper, nutmeg, and basil. Stir in the cheeses and vegetables. Spray a 9-inch deep-dish pie pan with nonstick vegetable spray or rub with a small amount of oil. Pour batter into the prepared dish.
4. On a gas grill, turn one burner to medium and the other one off; place the dish on the "off" side of the grill. In a kettle grill, move all the coals to one side and place the dish on the opposite side. Test the heat with

your hand to determine if it is about medium. If the grill is too hot, raise the baking dish with a brick or raise the grill away from the coals (if you have that option). Check after 10 minutes and turn the pan for even heat. Bake for 25 to 35 minutes. This can also be baked in a 350-degree oven for 25 to 30 minutes. Allow frittata to cool for at least 10 minutes before cutting. Serve hot or at room temperature.

MAKES 6 TO 8 SERVINGS.

Pasta

Fettuccine with Roasted Tomatoes and Garlic

This pasta dish with roasted tomatoes is ecstasy for garlic lovers. It makes an easy dinner on a hot summer night.

5 medium-large garden-ripe
tomatoes
Boiling salted water
8 ounces fettuccine, uncooked
⅓ cup olive oil
7 to 9 large cloves garlic,
minced
¼ cup loosely packed chopped
fresh basil, or 2 teaspoons
dry crumbled basil

¾ teaspoon salt
⅛ teaspoon freshly ground
black pepper
⅛ teaspoon crushed red
pepper
Freshly grated Parmesan
cheese

1. Preheat a gas grill to medium-hot or light a fire in a charcoal grill.
2. Cut tomatoes in half and place on the grill until they are browned well on all edges and oozing with juice. Set aside to cool.
3. Cook noodles in boiling water according to package directions. Drain.
4. Add olive oil to a medium-sized saucepan. Sauté the garlic, basil, salt, and peppers, stirring, until the oil bubbles gently and the garlic is light gold, about 2 to 3 minutes.
5. When tomatoes have cooled enough to handle, slip off the skins and discard. Add the tomatoes to the saucepan and mash with a potato masher. Heat through. Place noodles in a warm serving bowl and pour sauce over them. Toss gently. Pass the Parmesan at the table.

MAKES 4 SERVINGS.

Garden Grilled Vegetables
with Fusilli Pasta
and Parmesan

This is our family's favorite summer meal—pasta very primavera. When the garden is overflowing with ripe vegetables, we grill whatever is available.

12 ounces fusilli
   or other medium-size pasta

3 medium-size summer
   squashes (a variety of yellow
   zucchini and sunburst types)

1 medium-size red onion

1 small eggplant

2 bell peppers, any color

2 tablespoons extra-virgin
   olive oil

2 tablespoons balsamic vinegar

6 Roma tomatoes
   or 4 medium-size tomatoes

½ cup sliced black
   or Kalamata olives

3 to 5 cloves garlic, minced

½ teaspoon salt

⅛ teaspoon freshly grated black
   pepper

½ cup chopped fresh
   basil leaves

1 tablespoon chopped fresh
   thyme leaves

2 tablespoons vegetable broth
   or red wine (if necessary)

¼ cup freshly grated Parmesan
   cheese

½ cup grated mozzarella
   or Bel Paese cheese

1. Preheat a gas grill to hot or build a fire in a kettle grill.
2. In a large pot, cook pasta according to package directions. Drain and return to the pan.
3. Cut summer squashes in half lengthwise and slice ½ inch thick. Slice red onion and eggplant ½ inch thick. Cut peppers in half and remove the seeds and inner membrane. Brush the cut sides of vegetables with the olive oil and balsamic vinegar.

4. Place the whole tomatoes on the warming rack of a gas grill or on the outer edges of the kettle grill where heat is more moderate. Roast until softened and beginning to ooze juice. Remove them and set aside to cool. Remove the skins of the tomatoes in a separate bowl so as not to lose their juices; mash them with a potato masher. Add tomatoes to the pot containing pasta.

5. Grill the eggplant, squashes, and onion, turning occasionally, until tender but still firm: approximately 8 to 10 minutes for the squashes and onion and 8 to 12 minutes for the eggplant. Grill the peppers, turning occasionally, until evenly charred all over, about 8 to 10 minutes. Place peppers in a plastic bag until cool enough to touch, then peel off the skin. Remove other vegetables and set aside.

6. While grilled vegetables cool, add the olives, garlic, salt, pepper, basil, and thyme to the pasta. Dice all grilled vegetables to bite-size pieces and add to the pasta pot. Rewarm pasta and vegetables, adding 2 tablespoons broth or red wine if more liquid is needed. Add grated cheeses and warm through until melted.

MAKES 4 TO 6 SERVINGS.

Fusilli with Grilled Asparagus and Canellini Beans

This pasta dish is primarily assembled on the stove, but it features the smoky flavors of grilled asparagus and tomatoes.

1 pound asparagus	¼ cup chopped fresh basil
3 medium-size tomatoes	1 tablespoon fresh oregano
10 ounces fusilli, uncooked	or 1 teaspoon dried oregano
½ pound mushrooms	1 teaspoon salt
6 large green onions,	½ teaspoon freshly ground
top third of greens trimmed	black pepper
3 tablespoons olive oil	1 4-ounce can pitted sliced
4 to 6 cloves garlic, finely	black olives
chopped	1 15-ounce can canellini beans
¾ cup well-flavored vegetable	1 tablespoon cornstarch
stock (cubes are OK)	Freshly grated Parmesan
½ cup dry white wine	cheese

1. Preheat a gas grill or make a medium-hot fire in a kettle grill or use an existing fire after cooking other foods.
2. Trim the ends of the asparagus. Cut tomatoes in half. Place the asparagus on the grill for 8 to 10 minutes, turning or rolling every 2 minutes. Place the tomatoes at the edges of the grill and roast 10 to 12 minutes. Remove and set aside.
3. In a large stockpot, cook pasta according to package directions. While pasta cooks, prepare and slice mushrooms and green onions. Drain pasta in a colander and set aside.

4. In the same pan used for pasta, heat the oil and add the garlic. Sauté for 2 minutes and add the mushrooms and green onions. Sauté a few minutes before adding ½ cup of the vegetable broth, wine, basil, oregano, salt, and pepper. Trim asparagus to 1-inch pieces and add to the pan. Slip off the tomato skins (once grilled, the skins come off very easily). Mash tomatoes with a potato masher and add to the pan. Add the olives and canellini beans.

5. Mix together the cornstarch and remaining ¼ cup of broth in a small cup until smooth. Pour this into the stockpot. Bring to a boil, stirring constantly, until the sauce thickens, about 2 to 3 minutes.

6. Return the fusilli to the pan to heat through. Toss gently to mix well. Serve in a warm, shallow serving bowl. Pass the Parmesan cheese at the table.

MAKES 6 TO 8 SERVINGS.

Fusilli
with Roasted Peppers

The smoky sweetness of sun-infused peppers makes a classic summer evening entrée. Serve it with your own Focaccia on the Grill (see page 98).

3 sweet red peppers

3 sweet yellow or green peppers

12 ounces fusilli pasta, uncooked

½ cup sliced fresh basil leaves

2 to 3 tablespoons balsamic vinegar

2 tablespoons extra-virgin olive oil

¾ teaspoon salt

¼ teaspoon freshly ground pepper

2 medium-size tomatoes, diced

½ cup sliced Kalamata olives

4 ounces feta cheese, crumbled

1. Preheat a gas grill to medium or build a fire in a kettle grill.
2. Cut peppers in half, removing seeds and inner membrane. Place peppers on the heated grill and roast, covered, for 8 to 12 minutes, turning every few minutes, until evenly charred. Remove from the grill and place in a plastic bowl with a lid. Set aside to finish cooking and cool.
3. Cook pasta according to package directions; drain and set aside.
4. When peppers have cooled, peel off as much of the skin as you can and slice flesh into strips; reserve the pepper liquid. Using the same pot that you used for the pasta, combine all the vegetables, including the pepper strips and their juices, basil, balsamic vinegar, olive oil, salt, pepper, tomatoes, and olives; toss well. Heat through for 1 to 2 minutes.
5. Return the pasta to the pan and simmer a few more minutes until heated through, tossing gently. Sprinkle with feta cheese before serving or serve it separately at the table.

MAKES 6 SERVINGS.

Potato Main Dishes

�֎ Jim and Renee's
Potato Packets Especialle

Perfect campfire or grill food. One or two of these packets of slightly charred vegetables and potatoes is tastebud ecstasy.

2 medium-size red onions, quartered and sliced

3 medium-size sweet peppers (a variety of colors) seeded and chopped

3 to 4 small summer squashes, cut in half lengthwise and sliced

6 to 10 cloves garlic, finely chopped

¼ cup extra-virgin olive oil

¼ cup loosely packed chopped basil

2 tablespoons chopped fresh thyme

1 tablespoon chopped fresh rosemary (optional)

1 teaspoon salt

Generous grating of black pepper

6 to 7 medium-size baking potatoes, cut into bite-size pieces

½ to ⅔ cup water

Freshly grated Parmesan, feta cheese, or nutritional yeast

1. Prepare a medium-hot fire in a kettle grill or preheat a gas grill to medium.
2. Wash all vegetables thoroughly and cut to size. Place them in a large bowl along with the garlic, olive oil, herbs, salt, and pepper. Mix well with a large spoon.
3. Lay out double sheets of heavy-duty aluminum foil to make six individual packets. Cup the edges of the foil and add the potato/vegetable mixture to each packet. Add about 2 tablespoons water to each packet. Wrap

tightly. Lay the packets on the grill over a medium fire or cook them on a grill over a campfire. Depending on the hotness of the fire, they may take from 10 to 25 minutes to cook. Open a packet periodically to check if the potatoes are soft and beginning to caramelize on the bottom. Move the packets around the fire so that none is over a particularly hot spot. Open the packets and serve piping hot. Top with freshly grated Parmesan, crumbled feta cheese, or nutritional yeast.

MAKES 4 TO 5 SERVINGS.

Potatoes Alfredo

Yukon Gold potatoes, an especially buttery-flavored variety, are great in this recipe. They are available at farmers markets, natural-food stores, and some supermarkets.

5 to 6 medium-size thin-skinned potatoes	¾ teaspoon nutmeg
	¼ teaspoon salt
2 tablespoons butter	Generous grinding of
4 cloves garlic, minced	black pepper
½ cup low-fat milk	Nonstick vegetable cooking
⅓ cup grated Parmesan cheese	spray

1. Place potatoes in a large saucepan and cover with water. Bring to a boil. Reduce heat, cover, and simmer until potatoes are fork-tender but not mushy—about 15 minutes. Drain and cool.
2. Prepare a medium-hot fire in a kettle grill or preheat a gas grill.
3. In a small saucepan, melt butter and sauté the garlic for 2 minutes. Add the milk, Parmesan, nutmeg, salt, and pepper. Simmer 2 to 3 minutes but do not boil. Remove from heat and set aside.
4. Spray an 8-inch square disposable aluminum pan with nonstick vegetable spray, or use a square baking dish kept for the grill. Slice the potatoes and lay half of them in the pan. Pour half the Alfredo sauce over this. Layer the remaining potatoes over the sauce, season with additional salt and pepper (optional), and pour on remaining sauce. Cover the pan tightly with aluminum foil. Prepare the grill for indirect heat and add the pan. Cook for about 15 minutes, shaking the pan occasionally or turning it to encourage even cooking. Remove the foil and cook an additional 5 minutes.

MAKES 4 SERVINGS.

Grains

❈ Bulgur and Beans

This simple bulgur dish can be made on the stovetop or in a skillet on the grill. Its simple flavors are great with grilled corn, soup, or a summer salad.

¾ cups raw bulgur
1 tablespoon olive oil
½ green pepper, chopped
1 10.5-ounce can of tomatoes
1 small zucchini, grated

¾ cup water
1 15-ounce can kidney beans, rinsed and drained
Pinch of cayenne
½ teaspoon salt

1. In a large skillet with a lid, cook bulgur in oil, stirring until golden brown, about 3 to 4 minutes.
2. Add remaining ingredients and bring to a boil. Cover and simmer for 5 to 10 minutes or until bulgur is chewy soft. Set aside for 5 minutes before serving.

MAKES 4 TO 6 SERVINGS.

❋ Sautéed Couscous
with Pine Nuts and Garlic

This basic couscous dish is easy to prepare and combines nicely to fill out a meal with Summer Vegetable Kabobs (see page 122), a gazpacho (see pages 176, 177), or other summer soup.

1 to 2 tablespoons extra-virgin olive oil	¼ teaspoon salt
½ cup pine nuts	¼ cup finely chopped fresh basil
2 to 3 cloves garlic, minced	1 tablespoon lemon juice (optional)
1 cup couscous	Freshly ground black pepper
1½ cups water or vegetable broth	

1. Heat oil in an 8-by-10-inch skillet with a lid. Sauté the pine nuts about 3 minutes or until the nuts begin to brown slightly. Add garlic and sauté an additional 2 minutes.
2. Add the couscous, water, salt, basil, and lemon juice to the pan. Stir and raise heat to bring to a boil. Lower heat immediately, cover, and simmer about 3 minutes, until couscous is fluffy and tender to the bite. (Watch it closely—it cooks quickly.)

MAKES 4 TO 6 SERVINGS.

Variation: Omit the garlic and basil and cook couscous with ½ cup walnuts, 2 tablespoons freshly squeezed lemon juice, and 2 teaspoons grated lemon zest.

✺ Grilled Lemon and Basil Ratatouille with Couscous

This ratatouille is very different from others in that it has a distinct lemon and basil flavor.

2 tablespoons extra-virgin olive oil	5 to 6 large cloves garlic, minced
1 tablespoon balsamic vinegar	¼ cup fresh lemon juice
1 large eggplant, unpeeled, cut crosswise into ½-inch slices	Coarsely grated zest of one lemon
3 medium-size yellow crookneck or zucchini squash, cut lengthwise in strips about ¾ inch thick	¼ teaspoon salt
	¼ teaspoon freshly ground black pepper
1 large yellow onion, cut into ½-inch slices	¼ cup chopped fresh Italian parsley
2 cups firmly packed whole basil leaves	Freshly grated Parmesan cheese or nutritional yeast

1. Build a fire in a kettle grill or preheat a gas grill.
2. Place the olive oil and balsamic vinegar in a small bowl. Brush each slice of eggplant and squash with the oil/vinegar. Lightly brush the preheated grill with vegetable oil and place the eggplant, squash, and onion on it. Grill the vegetables, turning occasionally, until lightly charred and fork-tender—about 8 to 12 minutes for eggplant and onion and 8 to 10 minutes for the squash. Remove from grill and set aside to cool.
3. Mince the basil. Add the garlic, lemon juice, lemon zest, salt, and pepper to a 2-quart baking dish. When cooled, cube eggplant and squash into

1-inch bite-size pieces. Dice the onion. Add these vegetables to the basil mixture and toss to mix. Cover with aluminum foil and return to the grill. Bake over indirect heat at medium-high for 15 to 20 minutes. Uncover and add the chopped parsley; cook an additional 10 minutes.
4. Serve over couscous either hot or at room temperature. Top with a spoonful of freshly grated Parmesan or nutritional yeast.

MAKES 8 SERVINGS.

To Cook Couscous: Add 1 cup couscous to 1½ cups water and ¼ teaspoon salt in a small saucepan. Bring to a boil, cover, and simmer for 3 to 4 minutes. Stir once so couscous will not burn on the bottom. Remove from the stove and allow couscous to stand covered for 5 minutes before serving.

Paella

Paella is one of Spain's gastronomic glories. Its ingredients vary according to the region and catch (or harvest) of the day. If you are not a strict vegetarian, the addition of 1½ cups shrimp and/or other fish is traditional.

Paellas were first made, legend tells us, by field-workers who could not go home for lunch in the farmlands around Valencia. Paellas are still cooked over an open fire in Spain, and they work well on a charcoal or gas grill.

Most Spanish chefs agree that a good paella requires a paellera, a flat-bottomed shallow pan with sloping sides. You can, however, use a large cast-iron skillet or a flat-bottomed wok.

❀ Grilled Vegetable Paella

6 cups vegetable stock (cubes are OK)

½ teaspoon saffron threads

3 to 4 Roma tomatoes or 2 other larger, juicier tomatoes

1 cup frozen artichoke hearts, thawed

¾ cup green beans, fresh or frozen

2 medium-size summer squash, sliced lengthwise

1 medium-size green or yellow pepper, cut in half

3 tablespoons extra-virgin olive oil

1 small red onion, quartered and sliced

3 cloves garlic, minced

1½ cups Arborio rice (use a medium-grain rice if Arborio is not available)

¼ teaspoon salt

⅛ teaspoon freshly ground black pepper

¼ teaspoon paprika, preferably Spanish

1. Prepare a fire in a kettle grill or preheat a gas grill to high.
2. Combine stock and saffron in a saucepan. Bring to a boil. Cover and set aside. Return to boiling before adding to the paella.
3. Dice tomatoes and set aside. Slice artichoke hearts in half and cut green beans into 1-inch slices. Set aside separate from the tomatoes.
4. Add summer squashes and pepper to the grill. Grill on high temperature for 4 to 5 minutes each side. Leave the pepper on the grill until the outside is evenly charred. Place grilled peppers in a tightly sealed plastic bag until cool enough to handle. Then remove skin and cut pepper into 1-inch bite-size pieces.
5. Add olive oil to a paellera, cast-iron skillet, or other skillet with handles

that can be used on the grill. Add onion and garlic; sauté 3 to 5 minutes or until slightly caramelized. Add the rice to the pan and sauté 1 to 2 minutes more.

6. Pour in about a third of the boiling broth mixture and stir. Add the cut-up peppers and squashes, tomatoes, salt, pepper, and paprika. As stock is absorbed, replenish with additional boiling stock until rice is tender. Add green beans and artichokes the last 5 minutes of cooking. Remove from heat, cover the paella with a clean dish towel, and let rest for 5 minutes before serving. Add additional salt and pepper to taste. Serve hot or at room temperature.

MAKES 6 TO 8 SERVINGS.

4 ✳ CHAPTER

Burgers, Fries, and Other Traditional Fare

MANY VEGETARIANS, INCLUDING MYSELF, NEVER REALLY MISS meat . . . except when that wonderful smoky smell comes out of backyards everywhere. It makes me long for something from the barbecue.

There are now many varieties of vegetable burgers on the market. Some try to mimic the taste of beef and some have a distinct flavor of their own. Because they are so much lower in fat than meat, many do not hold together on the grill very well. They are best cooked in a vegetable grilling basket. A pizza warming pan that has holes in it also works well to manage more delicate burgers.

A variety of sensational burgers and sandwiches that have that smoky sweetness of grilling are included in this chapter. Potatoes—roasted, grilled, and in salads—are also included, and a barbecue book wouldn't be complete without barbecued beans.

Burgers, Dogs, and Other Sandwiches

Nut Burgers

This nut burger recipe is easy and tastes great. The recipe was given to me by the folks at the South Pine Street Cafe in Nevada City, California. I have adapted it slightly to help it hold together better on the grill.

3 tablespoons ground walnuts

3 tablespoons ground peanuts

2 egg whites

2 tablespoons grated cheddar cheese

2 tablespoons grated Monterey Jack cheese

¼ cup cooked brown short-grain rice

2 tablespoons whole-wheat flour

¼ teaspoon salt

Freshly grated black pepper

2 hamburger buns

1. Build a fire in a kettle grill or preheat a gas grill to medium-high.
2. Grind nuts in a food processor or blender and add to a bowl. Add all remaining ingredients. Make two patties with your hands. Place on a pizza warming pan and grill about 4 to 5 minutes per side.
3. Warm the buns on the grill for about 1 minute before serving and add your favorite accompaniments—tomato, mustard, lettuce, red onions, ketchup, the works.

MAKES 2 SERVINGS.

❋ Portobello Burgers
with Herb Mayonnaise

Portobello mushrooms and the smoky flavor of the grill form a happy taste marriage, a most delicious burger. Try using tofunnaise, a tofu-based mayonnaise spread.

⅓ cup mayonnaise or tofunnaise
1 clove garlic, minced
1 tablespoon chopped fresh thyme or basil
1 tablespoon lemon juice
Vegetable oil to brush on grill
2 slices of red onion, about ⅓ inch thick
2 thick slices of tomato, grilled

2 portobello mushrooms, stems removed
Olive oil or Teriyaki Sauce (page 143)
Salt and freshly ground black pepper
2 hamburger buns
Lettuce leaves

1. Build a fire in a kettle grill or preheat a gas grill to medium-hot.
2. In a small bowl, stir together the mayonnaise, garlic, thyme or basil, and lemon juice. Set aside.
3. Brush the grill with oil and add the slices of red onion. Grill the onions until softened and brown around the edges, about 10 to 12 minutes. Grill tomato slices 2 to 3 minutes. Brush the portobello mushrooms with a small amount of olive oil or Teriyaki Sauce. Grill mushrooms about 6 to 8 minutes per side or until softened and evenly charred. Season with salt and pepper. Grill buns, cut side down, until warmed, about 1 to 2 minutes.

4. Spread each bun with the herb mayonnaise and add the mushrooms. Top with the grilled onion, a slice of tomato, and lettuce if desired.

MAKES 2 SERVINGS.

Variation: Crumble a mellow blue cheese like Stilton or Gorgonzola onto the warmed bun before adding the portobello. Top with leaves of a mesclun mix of greens instead of lettuce for a more perky flavor.

Bulgur Burgers

This burger has an intriguing flavor. Serve it as a sandwich or as a pattie with the cucumber sauce.

1 cucumber, seeded, peeled, and grated	2 teaspoons coriander
½ cup plain low-fat yogurt	¼ teaspoon salt
2 teaspoons dill	Pinch of cayenne
1 tablespoon rice vinegar	3 cloves garlic, minced
⅛ teaspoon salt	¼ cup chopped fresh parsley
¾ cup water	2 tablespoons tahini
¾ cup raw bulgur	1 15-ounce can garbanzo beans, drained
2 tablespoons lemon juice	2 tablespoons whole-wheat or white flour
2 tablespoons olive oil	1 large egg plus 1 egg white, lightly beaten
¼ cup finely diced green onion	Vegetable oil
2 tablespoons chopped pistachios	6 hamburger buns
2 teaspoons cumin	

1. Combine cucumber, yogurt, dill, vinegar, and salt in a small bowl; cover and set aside.
2. In a small saucepan with a lid, bring water to a boil and add the bulgur and lemon juice. Cover and turn heat down; simmer for 5 to 6 minutes. Check to see if bulgur is tender to the bite and all water is absorbed. Set aside with the lid on to continue steaming.
3. Heat the olive oil in a large nonstick skillet over medium-heat. Add the green onion, pistachios, cumin, coriander, salt, cayenne, and garlic; sauté

2 minutes or until green onions are tender. Remove from heat and add the parsley and tahini.

4. Place garbanzo beans in a food processor; process until ground. In a large bowl combine garbanzos, green onion mixture, and bulgur; toss. Add the flour and beaten eggs; stir to combine well. Divide mixture into 6 equal portions, shaping into 3-inch patties.

5. Oil a vegetable basket or a pizza warming pan; grill the burgers 3 to 5 minutes on each side or until browned. Brush hamburger buns with olive oil and place on the warming rack of the grill or to the side where heat is lower. Place burgers on buns and top each with 2 to 3 table-spoons of the reserved cucumber sauce, a slice of tomato, lettuce, or other condiments you prefer.

MAKES 6 SERVINGS.

Teriyaki Tofu Steaks or Burgers

1 pound extra-firm tofu,
  well drained and pressed
  (see instructions on page 31)
¼ cup sake or sherry
2 tablespoons dark sesame oil
¼ cup soy sauce

2 tablespoons rice vinegar
2 large cloves garlic, minced
3 green onions, finely sliced
1 tablespoon honey
1 teaspoon cornstarch
  or arrowroot

1. Cut tofu into 6 equal ½-inch strips or into 6 patties 1 inch thick.
2. In a shallow bowl, combine sake or sherry, sesame oil, soy sauce, vinegar, garlic, green onions, and honey. Add the tofu and marinate in the refrigerator at least 12 hours.
3. Preheat a gas grill or build a fire in a kettle grill.
4. Place marinated tofu steaks/patties in a grill basket or on a screen. Grill tofu over medium-hot coals until browned and slightly crispy on both sides.
5. Add cornstarch or arrowroot to the leftover marinade sauce. Bring to a boil in a small saucepan and simmer for 2 minutes. Spoon over tofu steaks, if desired.

MAKES 3 TO 4 SERVINGS.

❦ Dogs Deluxe

Even the thought of a tofu dog makes some people look longingly toward the exit, but my children eat them with a passion. They don't hold together on a stick or on the grill very well, so I cook them in a vegetable basket. For the best flavor and a less rubbery texture, look for varieties that are *not* low-fat.

6 tofu dogs
6 whole-wheat hot dog buns
  Vegetable oil
1 small onion, sliced ⅓ inch
  thick

Accompaniments: Ketchup, mustard, pickles, relish

1. Preheat a gas grill or build a fire in a kettle grill.
2. When the fire is hot, lay the hot dogs in a vegetable grilling basket that has been lightly oiled. Grill dogs until evenly charred on all sides. Place buns on the edges of the grill for 1 to 2 minutes to warm through.
3. Serve hot dogs on buns and pass around all the fixings.

MAKES 4 TO 6 SERVINGS.

Pesto Grilled Cheese

My children love any excuse to eat pesto, and grilled cheeses are always favored fare. Slip in a tomato or grilled pepper on this sandwich—they may even eat it! This recipe calls for "tofurella," a tofu version of mozzarella. If you haven't sampled it lately, try again. It's getting better. It melts well, but the flavor is still a little flat. It's another opportunity to use more soy foods in the diet.

1 to 2 tablespoons pesto (pages 151, 152)
2 slices of your favorite sandwich bread
2 ounces tofurella, sliced ½ inch thick

1 tomato slice
1 grilled green pepper slice, about 2 to 3 inches wide

1. Spread pesto on one side of bread. Add the tofurella, tomato, and the grilled pepper.
2. Place sandwich in a vegetable grilling basket or directly on the grill. Grill on both sides until browned and cheese is melted.

MAKES 1 SANDWICH.

Beans

Barbecued Beans and Franks

¾ pound pinto beans
  (12 ounces)
6 cups cold water
¾ teaspoon salt
2 tablespoons vegetable oil
1 large onion, coarsely
  chopped
½ large sweet green pepper
  (seeds and membrane
  removed), cubed
3 cloves garlic, minced
1 package tofu dogs,
  cut in 1-inch pieces

3 to 4 tablespoons tomato
  paste
¾ cup ketchup
¾ teaspoon chili powder
¼ cup packed brown sugar
1½ teaspoons dry mustard
2 teaspoons white vinegar
½ teaspoon salt
¼ teaspoon freshly ground
  black pepper

1. Rinse beans and soak in cold water overnight. As an alternative, bring beans and cold water to a boil in a large saucepan; reduce heat and simmer uncovered for 2 minutes. Remove from heat; cover, and let stand for 1 hour.

2. Bring beans to a boil in that same pan; reduce heat and simmer, covered, for 1½ hours or until beans are soft but not mushy. Add salt the last 20 minutes of cooking. Tip pot to drain beans, reserving 2 cups of the liquid.

3. Preheat a gas grill or use an existing fire in a kettle grill.

4. Return 1½ cups of the liquid to the pot, reserving remaining liquid; return pot to heat.

5. Meanwhile, in a large skillet or medium-saucepan, heat oil over medium-high; sauté onion, green pepper, and garlic for 5 to 8 minutes or until vegetables are softened. Add hot dog pieces along with the tomato paste, ketchup, chili powder, brown sugar, mustard, vinegar, salt, and pepper. Bring to a boil for 1 to 2 minutes. Remove from heat. Add mixture to the beans.

6. Place pot of beans on the barbecue when coals have burnt down to a medium temperature. Simmer uncovered for 15 to 20 minutes or until beans and vegetables are tender, adding some of the reserved cooking liquid if beans become dry. Taste and adjust seasoning.

MAKES 8 TO 10 SERVINGS.

Grandmother's Baked Beans (But Better)

This dish brings back memories of picnics and family reunions when I was a child. It uses several meat substitutes. Stripples are a low-fat bacon made of textured soy protein and grains, and soy links are a breakfast sausage made of the same. Seitan is wheat gluten that has a similar texture of meat. They are available at natural food grocery stores and some supermarkets.

If you have a grill that has a reliable low heat, cook this in a large stockpot, but it is best done in a crockpot or on the stove at a low temperature.

1 large onion, chopped	1 16-ounce can butter lima beans or garbanzo beans, drained
1 8-ounce package Stripples vegetarian bacon strips	
1 8-ounce package soy links or 8 ounces seitan, cut into 1-inch pieces	1 16-ounce can kidney beans, drained and rinsed
3 16-ounce cans vegetarian baked beans	1 cup ketchup
	3 tablespoons white or apple cider vinegar
	2 teaspoons liquid smoke
	¼ cup brown sugar

1. Sauté onion in a frying pan. Remove to a large bowl. Using the same pan, sauté the vegetarian bacon 4 to 5 minutes on each side. Sauté the soy links 4 to 5 minutes total. Set aside to cool; cut into bite-size pieces.

2. In the same bowl as the onions, add the bacon and soy links, beans, ketchup, vinegar, liquid smoke, and sugar. Transfer this to a crockpot and cook on high for about 4 hours, stirring occasionally. Or simmer it for 1 to 2 hours in a large stockpot on the stove.

MAKES 8 TO 10 SERVINGS.

Potatoes and Fries

❄ Potatoes from the Coals

This is a great way to cook potatoes. You can place them on the edge of the grill while other foods are cooking.

2 tablespoons olive oil

2 medium-size onions, quartered and sliced

4 cloves garlic, chopped or minced

3 to 4 sprigs fresh thyme, about 2 inches long

Salt and a generous grating of black pepper

1½ pounds Yukon Gold or other thin-skinned potato, cut into 1-inch pieces (new red potatoes are a great size)

¼ cup water

1. Preheat a gas grill to medium-high or build a fire in a kettle grill.
2. Combine olive oil, onions, garlic, thyme, salt, and pepper in a large mixing bowl. Add the cut-up potatoes and toss with your hands to mix.
3. Lay out 2 to 3 layers of aluminum foil large enough to hold the potatoes. Add the potato/onion mixture to the center of the foil. Add the water and fold it up so that the potatoes are wrapped firmly. Place foil packet on the edge of the grill where heat is more moderate, and cook about 35 to 50 minutes. Check halfway through the cooking: Potatoes should be softened and starting to caramelize but not burnt.

MAKES 6 TO 8 SERVINGS.

❉ Roasted Potato Wedges

You won't convince the kids these are anything close to french fries, but once they add that miracle substance—ketchup—they'll love them just the same. Precooking the potatoes until barely crisp-tender (about 10 minutes) shortens their time on the grill slightly. If you plan to have guests, this task can be done ahead of time to simplify the last-minute cooking.

2 tablespoons olive oil
or Garlic Oil (page 160)
Salt and freshly ground black
pepper
1 tablespoon minced fresh
parsley (optional)

1 tablespoon minced fresh
thyme (optional)
4 to 6 medium-size baking
potatoes, washed and cut
into 8 wedges
(peel if desired)

1. Preheat a grill to medium-high or use an existing fire.
2. Combine olive oil or Garlic Oil, salt, pepper, parsley, and thyme in a shallow baking dish. Add potato wedges. Using your hands, cover each potato with oil and herbs as much as you can.
3. Place potatoes directly on the grill and cover. Roast for 25 to 30 minutes, turning occasionally.

MAKES 4 TO 6 SERVINGS.

Variation: For more sophisticated tastes, brush the potatoes with Olive Tapenade (page 162) or Barbecue Sauce (page 150) while cooking.

❋ Sweet Potato Corn Cakes

2 pounds sweet potatoes
   or yams
½ cup diced red bell pepper
½ cup fresh or frozen corn
2 tablespoons finely diced
   parsley
4 to 6 green onions or chives,
   diced finely

¾ teaspoon salt
¼ to ½ teaspoon freshly ground
   black pepper
¼ teaspoon nutmeg or mace
   (optional)
Vegetable oil

1. In an oven, bake the sweet potatoes at 350 degrees Fahrenheit until flesh is soft but not mushy—about 40 minutes. Set aside to cool.
2. Preheat a gas grill or use an existing fire in a kettle grill.
3. When potatoes are cool, scoop out flesh into a large bowl. Add the bell pepper, corn, parsley, green onions, salt, pepper, and nutmeg. With your hands, shape the mixture into cakes about 3 inches in diameter and about ½ inch thick.
4. Generously oil a pizza warming pan and preheat it on the grill. Add the sweet potato cakes to the pan and grill about 1 to 2 minutes on each side.

MAKES 4 TO 6 SERVINGS.

Potato
Salads

Greek Style
Potato Salad

I use raw green beans in this simple potato salad. Fresh-picked from the garden or from the farmers' market, they are great raw. Most beans available in grocery stores are harvested a little too late, when the inner seed pod is more developed. If this is what you have available, you may want to steam them for a few minutes.

5 to 6 medium-size thin-skinned red potatoes or Yukon Gold potatoes

½ pound green beans, broken into 1-inch pieces

4 ounces Kalamata olives, pitted and sliced

1 small red onion, quartered and sliced thinly

3 Roma tomatoes, cut up

¼ to ⅓ cup Herb Vinaigrette (page 145)

2 ounces feta cheese, crumbled

1. Wash and cut potatoes in half. In a medium-size saucepan with a lid, cook potatoes in a small amount of water until softened but not mushy, about 8 to 12 minutes.

2. In a large bowl, combine the green beans, olives, red onion, and tomatoes. When potatoes have cooled enough to handle, cut into bite-size pieces and add to the salad. Blend in the Herb Vinaigrette. Crumble feta cheese on top and serve.

MAKES ABOUT 4 TO 6 SERVINGS.

❋ Roasted Pepper and Potato Salad

Cilantro and lime juice create a distinctive flavor for this potato salad.

7 cups cubed unpeeled Yukon Gold potatoes (about 3 pounds)

3 large bell peppers (about 1½ pounds), a variety of colors

1 bunch green onions, sliced

¾ cup finely chopped cilantro

¼ cup thinly sliced shallot

⅓ cup freshly squeezed lime juice

¾ teaspoon salt

⅛ teaspoon freshly ground black pepper

½ teaspoon white pepper

2 to 3 tablespoons extra-virgin olive oil

1. Preheat a gas grill to high or build a fire in a kettle grill.
2. Place potato cubes in a large saucepan. Add enough water to cover potatoes and bring to a boil. Cover, reduce heat, and simmer 8 to 10 minutes or until potatoes are tender. Drain and set aside.
3. Cut bell peppers in half lengthwise; discard seeds and membranes. Place peppers on the preheated grill, turning occasionally, until evenly charred all over. Place peppers in a plastic bag and seal; let stand 15 minutes. Peel and discard skins; cut peppers into 1-inch pieces.
4. Combine potato, peppers, green onions, cilantro, and shallot in a large bowl; toss gently, and set aside. Combine lime juice, salt, pepper, and olive oil in a separate bowl; mix to combine and pour over the potato mixture. Toss gently, cover, and chill. The flavors in this salad taste best if allowed to chill for 1 to 2 hours.

MAKES 8 TO 10 SERVINGS.

Potato and Feta Cheese Salad with Fresh Herbs

The vibrant flavor of this potato salad is worth the extra time it takes to assemble. It's a meal in itself.

1½ pounds small red potatoes
¼ cup chopped fresh dill
2 tablespoons fresh oregano or
   1½ teaspoons dried
¼ cup chopped fresh parsley
3 tablespoons lemon juice
   ½-inch-thick slice of
   red onion
3 tablespoons extra-virgin
   olive oil
2 teaspoons grated lemon peel
2 tablespoons chopped
   fresh mint, or substitute
   1½ teaspoons dried or
   1 mint teabag

½ teaspoon salt
⅛ teaspoon cayenne (or less)
4 to 5 large green onions,
   thinly sliced
1 red pepper, diced
1 large tomato, chopped
1 cucumber, peeled and diced
½ small to medium-size head
   of romaine lettuce, cut into
   strips
10 to 12 Kalamata olives, pitted
   and sliced
6 ounces feta cheese, crumbled
   Garnish: Dill sprigs or lemon
   wedges (optional)

1. Cook potatoes in boiling salted water in a medium-size saucepan until just tender, about 15 minutes. Drain and cool.
2. Add oregano, parsley, lemon juice, red onion, oil, lemon peel, mint, salt, and cayenne to a blender or food processor. Puree until dressing is as smooth as possible. (Dressing can be prepared a day ahead.)

3. Cut potatoes into bite-size pieces. Transfer to a large bowl. Pour dressing over warm potatoes and toss together.

4. Add the green onions, red pepper, tomato, cucumber, lettuce, olives, and cheese to potatoes and toss together. Mound salad on plates. Garnish with dill sprigs or lemon wedges. Serve at room temperature.

MAKES 8 TO 12 SERVINGS.

Bruschettas, Pizzas, and Breads on the Grill

MOST OF US HAVE A LIMITED CONCEPT OF WHAT WE CAN COOK on the grill. Grills can perform a much wider range of cooking activities than we generally use them for. If you learn how to create an indirect source of heat on the grill, you can make desserts, bake casseroles, slow-roast vegetables, and even bake your own breads outdoors, where the heat won't make the kitchen feel like the inside of an oven.

Bruschettas

Bruschettas are an Italian appetizer made of toasted bread that is traditionally rubbed with garlic, tomatoes, and olive oil. These variations are simple to prepare, nutritious, and a great way to use an abundance of summer produce. Use bruschettas as an accompaniment to a summer soup, salad, or pasta—or as a simple meal in themselves.

Tomato Bruschettas

6 to 8 Roma tomatoes
   or 3 large tomatoes
3 tablespoons capers
2 tablespoons extra-virgin
   olive oil
1 cup loosely packed basil
   leaves

3 to 4 cloves garlic
   Dash of salt
1 loaf sourdough
   or sweet French bread
   Freshly grated Parmesan
   cheese

1. Preheat a gas grill to medium-high or use an existing fire in a kettle grill.
2. Place first six ingredients in a blender or food processor. Blend but do not liquefy.
3. Cut bread into thick slices and toast on the grill 2 to 3 minutes each side. Remove and spoon tomato mixture on top of each slice; add cheese if desired. Return to the grill for a few minutes. (A pizza warming pan is convenient for moving the bread slices on and off the grill.)

MAKES 8 TO 10 SERVINGS AS AN APPETIZER.

Bruschetta
with Mushrooms

1 baguette or 4 to 6 slices French bread
Olive oil to brush on bread
½ pound mushrooms, sliced (about 2 cups)
2 tablespoons extra-virgin olive oil
¼ cup finely chopped fresh basil
Salt and freshly ground black pepper
⅓ cup freshly grated Parmesan cheese
3 ripened tomatoes

1. Preheat a gas grill to medium-high or build a fire in a kettle grill.
2. Cut off a 12-inch piece of baguette and slice it lengthwise. Brush the inside of the bread lightly with olive oil. Put both halves, soft side up, on the grill 7 to 8 minutes, or until the outside is a bit crunchy but the inside is still soft.
3. Sauté the mushrooms in 2 tablespoons olive oil over medium-high heat until they begin to brown on the outside. Add the basil, salt, and pepper. Remove from heat. While the mushrooms are still warm but not hot, add the Parmesan and mix so that the cheese softens a bit.
4. Slice tomatoes about ¼ inch thick. Layer tomatoes on the bread. Place mushrooms on top of the tomatoes. Cut bread into 3-inch lengths and return to the grill just until heated through.

MAKES 6 TO 8 SERVINGS.

Roasted Pepper
and Garlic Bruschetta

1 sweet red pepper
1 sweet green pepper
1 sweet yellow pepper
1 head of garlic
2 tablespoons plus 1 teaspoon
extra-virgin olive oil
1 loaf French bread
or a baguette

2 tablespoons balsamic
or white wine vinegar
Salt and freshly ground black
pepper
3 ounces freshly grated
Parmesan cheese

1. Preheat a gas grill to medium-high or build a fire in a kettle grill.
2. Place whole peppers on the grill. Place head of garlic on sheet of aluminum foil, drizzle with 1 teaspoon olive oil, and fold up sides of foil to cover; place packet directly on the grill. Cover the grill and roast peppers 15 to 20 minutes, turning every 10 minutes. Remove from oven. Carefully place peppers in a tightly closed plastic bag; allow peppers to steam and cool—about 15 minutes. Remove garlic from the grill in 30 to 40 minutes.
3. Reduce grill temperature to medium. Cut bread into 8 slices, each about ½ inch thick. Place bread directly on the grill and toast for 6 to 8 minutes or until lightly browned.
4. When peppers are cool, cut in half and remove seeds and membranes. Peel away the charred skin of the peppers with your fingers; chop peppers finely. Peel garlic cloves and chop finely. Add peppers, garlic, 2 tablespoons oil, and vinegar to a small bowl. Toss to combine. Season with small amount of salt and pepper to taste.
5. Divide pepper mixture among slices of bread. Top with a small amount of Parmesan cheese and return to the grill to warm through (about 2 to 3 minutes).

MAKES 6 TO 8 SERVINGS.

Pizzas on the Grill

Plan a "Make Your Own Pizza Party" for a lively evening with friends. It's also a great teenage activity. Ask each person (or family) to bring certain ingredients: for example, pesto, tomato sauce, olives, mushrooms, cheeses, cut-up pineapple, washed and chopped spinach. Be sure to ask someone to bring an extra cutting board for rolling out dough.

When the guests arrive, have the dough ready to roll and put them to work. It's not a bad idea to have one pizza already made and some premade crusts available—especially if everyone has to wait for one grill to cook enough pizza for a crowd. Put kids and teenagers to work chopping vegetables and rolling dough. Be sure to have parents in charge of the actual grilling of the pizzas as it is not a safe activity for kids (even those who already know everything).

If you don't want to make your own pizza dough, there are lots of other options that make grilling pizza easy. Thin-crust Italian bread shells are available in most grocery stores (such as Boboli breads). A loaf of frozen bread dough can be cut in half and rolled out into two pizza shells. English muffins are also fun to use for mini pizzas.

Add mesquite or hardwood chips to the grill and you have the wonderful flavor of pizzas baked in wood-fired ovens that is so popular in restaurants around the country.

Pizza Dough

Make your own pizza dough? Sure you can! It's so easy you'll wonder why you didn't do it before. Pizza dough is best made with a combination of white and wheat flours. If you prefer a greater proportion of whole wheat, by all means add more.

- 1 envelope active dry yeast (2½ teaspoons)
- 1½ cups hot water
- 1 tablespoon olive oil
- 1 teaspoon salt
- 3 cups unbleached white flour
- 1 cup whole-wheat flour
- 2 tablespoons cornmeal (optional)
- Vegetable oil or nonstick vegetable cooking spray

1. Dissolve the yeast in ¼ cup of warm water (105–115 degrees Fahrenheit). When the yeast has softened and become foamy, in about 7 to 10 minutes, add the rest of the water, olive oil, and salt.
2. Measure the flours into a separate bowl and make a well in the center. Gradually stir the water and yeast into the well. Stir in as much of the flour as you can. Add cornmeal if desired.
3. Knead the dough on a lightly floured surface about 3 to 4 minutes or until smooth and elastic, adding more flour if needed. Place the dough in a bowl that has been lightly oiled or coated with nonstick spray. Cover dough with a clean cloth and let rise 1 hour or until it has doubled in size.
4. Punch dough down and work it into a smooth, round shape. Divide into two portions. Cover them with a damp towel until you are ready to use. Roll out dough but don't be too concerned if the circles are not perfectly round.

MAKES TWO 12-INCH PIZZAS—ONE FOR DINNER AND ONE TO FREEZE.

To Freeze Pizza Dough: After kneading it, divide into convenient portions, rub the dough with a small amount of oil, and pack into airtight freezer bags. Maximum storing time is about 3 months. Thaw it at room temperature at breakfast and have pizza for dinner that night.

Spinach and Feta Pizza

1 medium-size red onion,
  sliced ⅓-inch thick
1 Boboli bread pizza shell
  or 1 10-inch round of
  sourdough bread, top cut off
  (leaving a round base about
  1 inch thick)
¾ to 1 cup tomato sauce
  (homemade or store-bought)
6 ounces mozzarella cheese,
  sliced thinly

3 cups spinach, washed,
  spun dry, and finely chopped
½ cup crumbled feta cheese
½ 6-ounce jar of marinated
  artichoke hearts, each cut
  in half (optional)
½ cup pine nuts or chopped
  walnuts
5 to 6 large cloves garlic,
  chopped

1. Light a hot fire in a charcoal grill or preheat a gas grill to medium-high.
2. Place onion slices directly on the grill until softened and edges become charred. Toast both sides of the pizza shell on the grill for 2 to 3 minutes; remove.
3. Spread tomato sauce over entire top of pizza shell. Distribute mozzarella evenly over the sauce. Separate grilled onion into rings and add to the pizza. Spread spinach evenly over the pizza and add the feta cheese. Sprinkle with artichoke hearts, nuts, and chopped garlic.
4. Place pizza on a pizza warming pan and close grill lid. Grill until spinach is limp and cheese has melted—about 5 to 10 minutes. Return to a cutting board and cut into wedges.

MAKES 4 TO 6 SERVINGS.

Pesto Pizza with Tomatoes and Mozzarella

1 recipe Pizza Dough
  (pages 89–90)
½ to ¾ cup Basil Pesto
  (page 152)
2 to 3 medium-size tomatoes,
  mixture of red and yellow
Salt and freshly ground black
  pepper

½ small red onion, thinly sliced
3 ounces mozzarella,
  thinly grated
1 4-ounce can sliced black
  olives

1. Prepare the pizza dough and set it in a warm place to rise.
2. Light a hot fire in a charcoal grill or preheat a gas grill to medium-high.
3. Prepare the pesto.
4. Slice the tomatoes crosswise and season them with salt and pepper; set aside. When the grill is hot, place the sliced onion in a vegetable basket or pizza pan and grill on each side for 5 to 7 minutes or until softened and the edges are slightly brown.
5. On a floured surface, shape the dough into a circle approximately 10 inches in diameter and ¼ to ⅓ inch thick. Make a small edging by pinching up the dough with your fingers.
6. Slide the dough onto a lightly oiled pizza pan, top side down, and grill at medium-high temperature until it begins to bubble up and grill lines appear on the bottom—about 4 to 7 minutes. (To put this crust directly onto the grill, carry the whole cutting board to the grill and slide it on.) Carefully remove from the grill and turn dough to the other side.

7. Return to the kitchen and spread the pesto sauce onto the cooked side of the pizza dough; top with the grated mozzarella, sliced tomatoes, grilled onions, and olives.

8. Return pizza to the grill. Cook 5 to 7 more minutes or until the cheese is melted and the dough is cooked through. Watch carefully to make sure the underside is not burning. (You may want to close the lid of the grill.) When the crust is crisp and the toppings are warmed through, remove from the grill. Place on a cutting board and cut into wedges.

MAKES 4 TO 6 SERVINGS.

Grilled Garlic
and Arugula Pizza

2 tablespoons extra-virgin
olive oil or nonstick olive oil
cooking spray
4 to 6 cloves garlic, minced
½ pound mushrooms, sliced
3 to 4 plum tomatoes, chopped
3 cups arugula or a mixture
of arugula, spinach, and/or
escarole

1 10-inch thin-crust Italian
bread shell (such as Boboli)
or 1 round loaf of sourdough
bread, top cut off
(leaving a circle 1 inch thick)
½ cup crumbled feta cheese

1. Preheat a gas grill to medium-high or build a fire in a kettle grill.
2. Add olive oil to a large skillet and heat over medium heat. Add the garlic
   and mushrooms and sauté for 3 to 4 minutes. Add tomatoes and greens;
   stir to mix, cover, and steam about 4 minutes or until greens are wilted.
3. Brush both sides of the pizza crust with olive oil. Place the pizza crust
   either on a pizza pan made for the grill or on a piece of aluminum foil.
   Grill crust 2 to 3 minutes on each side.
4. Remove from the grill and add the sautéed vegetables and cheese to the
   pizza. Return to the grill, cover, and heat through 4 to 6 minutes. Cut
   into wedges to serve.

MAKES 4 TO 6 SERVINGS.

Mexican Pizzas
on the Grill

This fast and easy recipe is guaranteed to please kids—even really persnickety ones.

2 cups diced tomato
1 tablespoon minced fresh cilantro
4 to 5 green onions, finely chopped
½ teaspoon ground cumin
½ teaspoon garlic powder

1 tablespoon fresh lime juice
4 8-inch flour tortillas
1½ cups vegetarian refried beans
¾ cup shredded Monterey Jack or mozzarella cheese (about 3 ounces)

1. Combine tomato, cilantro, green onions, cumin, garlic powder, and lime juice in a bowl. Stir well, then set aside.
2. Heat tortillas on the grill at a medium-high temperature, until just crunchy—approximately 2 minutes on each side.
3. Spread approximately 6 tablespoons beans over each tortilla; top with ⅓ cup of the tomato mixture and 2 tablespoons of shredded cheese. Arrange pizzas on a cookie sheet or a pizza pan that will fit onto the grill; close cover. Grill 4 to 5 minutes or until tortillas are crisp and cheese melts; cut into wedges.

MAKES 4 SERVINGS.

Breads on the Grill

To make bread on the grill you will need to set up the grill for indirect heat. (See directions in chapter 2.) All grills are somewhat different and most have hot spots, so turn the bread when it is partially baked and watch it a little more closely than if you were baking it in an oven.

Basil Beer Bread

This simple-to-prepare bread is a great accompaniment for a platter of grilled vegetables or freshly sliced tomatoes.

Vegetable oil

3 cups self-rising flour

3 tablespoons sugar or
1 tablespoon honey

⅔ cup finely chopped basil, lightly packed

1½ cups warm beer

1. Preheat one burner of a gas grill to medium or build a fire in a kettle grill.
2. Lightly oil a 9-by-5-by-3-inch loaf pan. In a large bowl, combine flour, sugar, and basil. Slowly pour warm beer over dry ingredients and mix. Transfer dough to loaf pan.
3. Place loaf pan on the warming rack or the unheated burner of a gas grill for 40 to 45 minutes or until a knife comes out clean. Or set the charcoal grill up for indirect heat and bake. If the grill is too hot, remove the lid for a few minutes. Slice when bread has cooled slightly. This bread can also be baked in an oven at 350 degrees for 45 to 50 minutes.

MAKES ONE LOAF OF BREAD.

Focaccia
on the Grill

This focaccia bread requires only a single rising and is a pleasure to make as well as to eat. If you're using a charcoal grill, cook those foods that require the highest flame first, then arrange the coals for indirect heat. On a gas grill this bakes best on a warming rack at medium-high temperature; or arrange for indirect heat according to instructions in chapter 2.

1 package active dry yeast (2½ teaspoons)	Vegetable oil or nonstick vegetable cooking spray
1 cup warm water (105–115 degrees)	Olive oil for coating loaves Optional ingredients:
1 teaspoon salt	finely chopped grilled onion,
3 tablespoons extra-virgin olive oil	1 tablespoon chopped fresh herbs, ½ cup Kalamata olives,
1 teaspoon sugar	sun-dried tomatoes,
2½ cups unbleached white flour or a mixture of whole-wheat and white	or ¼ cup Parmesan cheese

1. Prepare a gas or kettle grill for indirect heat following instructions in chapter 2.
2. Dissolve the yeast in the warm water. After 2 to 3 minutes add the salt, olive oil, and sugar. Stir in the flour in small batches. Once the dough has been formed, turn it out onto a lightly floured board. Knead for a few minutes until the dough is smooth and shiny.
3. Place the dough in a lightly oiled bowl (or use a nonstick vegetable cook-

ing spray). Cover it with a clean towel and put it in a warm place to rise, about 30 to 40 minutes or until doubled in size.

4. Remove the dough from the bowl and punch down. At this point you can return the bread to the board to work in the additional ingredients if you desire. Shape the dough into two small loaves and rub with a light coating of olive oil. Cut two pieces of aluminum foil and place one loaf on each one, folding the foil loosely around the loaves.

5. Place breads on the grill for 20 to 25 minutes or until the bread is nicely browned. (You could also bake these in the top third of an oven 25 to 30 minutes at 375 degrees.) Serve warm from the oven, plain or with Garlic Oil (see page 160).

MAKES ONE LARGE OR TWO SMALL LOAVES OF BREAD.

Variation: Add about 1 tablespoon freshly chopped rosemary or other herbs to the dough. Press chopped Kalamata olives or sun-dried tomatoes into the dough after it has risen.

❈ Garlic Breadsticks

You can cut and prepare these breadsticks ahead of time. Then, at the last minute, they will be ready to grill and serve.

1 thin baguette or other crusty loaf	¼ cup Garlic Oil (page 160) or Roasted Garlic Paste (page 154)

1. Light a fire in the grill or use an existing one.
2. With a serrated knife, cut the loaf of bread into quarters lengthwise. If you use a regular-size loaf of French bread, you may want to cut it into more than four pieces. Brush the bread on all sides with the oil or paste.
3. Lay the bread quarters on the grill rack, cover, and grill, turning occasionally, until lightly browned on all sides—about 4 to 7 minutes altogether. Serve immediately.

MAKES 4 TO 6 SERVINGS.

Skillet Cornbread

The grill is a perfect place to prepare Skillet Cornbread. Preheat a well-greased cast-iron pan and bake covered to achieve a crisp brown crust. This bread is great with Barbecued Beans and Franks (page 70) or Grandmother's Baked Beans (page 72).

1 cup unbleached white or whole-wheat pastry flour	4 teaspoons baking powder
1 cup cornmeal	¾ teaspoon salt
¼ cup sugar or 2 tablespoons honey	1 egg or 2 egg whites
	1 cup milk
	2 tablespoons melted butter

1. Prepare a gas or kettle grill for indirect heat following instructions in chapter 2.
2. Sift together all the dry ingredients.
3. Beat the egg with the milk and add it to the flour mixture along with the melted butter. Stir to combine.
4. Spread the batter in a well-greased 10-inch cast-iron skillet or one that can be used on the grill. Cover with aluminum foil. (Remove foil for the last 10 minutes of baking.) Bake for about 20 to 30 minutes or until sides begin to pull away from the pan and bread is springy. Cool slightly before cutting.

MAKES 6 TO 8 SERVINGS.

Variation: Replace some of the sugar with molasses or add 2 teaspoons ground fennel or anise seeds.

Skillet Cornbread
with Jalapeños and Cheddar

If using fresh jalapeño peppers for this flavorful recipe, wear rubber gloves while chopping the peppers so that they will not burn tender skin or get on your fingers and into your eyes.

1 cup cornmeal	1 3-ounce can chili peppers
½ cup whole-wheat	or 1 fresh jalapeño pepper,
or all-purpose flour	seeded and minced
2 teaspoons baking powder	1 egg plus 1 egg white
¾ teaspoon baking soda	1 cup buttermilk
½ teaspoon salt	¼ cup butter, melted and
¾ cup grated sharp cheddar	cooled
cheese	Vegetable oil

1. Prepare a gas or kettle grill for indirect heat following instructions in chapter 2.
2. In a bowl, combine the cornmeal, flour, baking powder, baking soda, and salt. Add the cheddar and the jalapeño, and toss the mixture well.
3. In another bowl, whisk together the eggs, buttermilk, and melted butter. Add the egg mixture to the cornmeal mixture, and stir the batter until it is just combined.
4. Spread the batter in a well-greased 10-inch cast-iron skillet. Cover with aluminum foil. (Remove foil for the last 10 minutes of cooking.) Bake for 20 to 25 minutes, or until bread is springy to the touch and begins to pull away from the sides of the pan. Cool slightly before cutting.

MAKES 6 TO 8 SERVINGS.

6 ✳ CHAPTER

Vegetables on the Grill

SATURDAY IS MY FAVORITE DAY OF THE WEEK. AFTER AN EARLY-morning trip to the farmers' market visiting with neighbors and friends, I am enthusiastic about coming home to make a meal with locally grown produce. Buying fresh-picked produce creates a quality difference that reverberates throughout your whole life—bringing back a sense of community pride and appreciation of our abundant planet. Organically grown vegetables are free of the chemical residue found in commercial produce. The long-term benefits of organic farming both for our planet and for our individual health are just beginning to be understood.

Buying the freshest produce makes meal preparation simpler; the natural intense flavors need little embellishment. Every time I visit Chez Panisse in Berkeley, California, I am reminded of the validity of Alice Waters's cooking philosophy: Quality ingredients prepared simply are a winner nearly every time.

Until recently, we have relegated vegetables to the position of a side dish, but in this chapter you will find them at plate center—the main attraction in all their sun-saturated glory. They can be marinated and grilled and served with a simple dipping sauce, combined with pasta or grains, skewered as kabobs, and even roasted on the grill.

Tips for Grilling Vegetables

Grilling brings out the smoky sweetness of vegetables and doesn't overcomplicate their fresh-picked flavors. Almost any vegetable with a high water content can be successfully grilled. Mesquite is the flavored wood of choice for most vegetable dishes. However, if the dish is to remain on the grill for less than 5 minutes, flavored smoke does not make much of a difference.

Larger amounts of vegetables (and potatoes) are often foil-wrapped on the grill, a method that works well, but placing vegetables directly on the coals gives them a more smoky flavor. To grill vegetables, sear them over high heat, then move them to the edge of the grill to finish cooking over low heat. They must be monitored carefully, as only a few minutes can make the difference between nicely charred and still crunchy and blackened. This means no phone calls—let that answering machine do its job.

Some vegetables must be precooked or blackened before they soften enough to eat. They can either be blanched on top of the stove or microwaved for a few minutes. All vegetables that are precooked should be cooked just until a knife can pierce them. Artichokes, beets, broccoli (optional), sweet potatoes, and potatoes in some cases need to be precooked.

Many grilled vegetables and vegetable dishes are best served at room temperature, so you can grill them before friends arrive, leaving the grill available for other dishes.

The cut sides of some vegetables that are to be grilled need to be brushed with olive oil to avoid a dried-out look. I prefer to use a marinade of 2 tablespoons olive oil and 2 tablespoons balsamic vinegar. That way I use less fat. In most cases, brushing on the oil is the best (though somewhat more time-consuming) way to assure that you don't end up with oily-tasting vegetables. Eggplant, zucchini, corn, potatoes, and a few other vegetables are best if brushed with oil. Tomatoes, mushrooms, and onions require a short time on the grill and do not necessarily need to be brushed—thus cutting back on fat content even further.

Grilling times for vegetables are highly variable. It all depends on how hot the grill is and the size of the vegetables. Both of these factors can vary immensely. You must move vegetables around the grill, rolling and turning them. Use tongs or a large metal spatula to turn foods; forks puncture the surface and allow flavorful juices to drain away. When a fork can easily pierce them, they're done.

Grilling is not rocket science. Your own preferences and observations of what's cooked and not cooked are your best tools. The chart that follows gives some general guidelines, but your own sense of texture and color must be the ultimate determining factor.

Grilling Fresh Vegetables

VEGETABLE	SPECIAL PREPARATION	GRILLING TIME
Artichokes	Cut off top spikes, trim stem and outer leaves. Cook in boiling water until tender (25–40 minutes). Cut in half lengthwise to grill.	6–8 minutes
Beets	Best cooked whole at a slow-roast temperature.	35–45 minutes
Bell peppers	Core, remove seeds and membranes; cut in half or grill peppers whole.	8–10 minutes 15–20 minutes (whole)
Broccoli	Peel tough stalks and cut in half; cut into medium-size florets; blanch for 2–3 minutes (optional).	5–8 minutes
Carrots	Blanch carrots in boiling water to cover, about 5–7 minutes, unless you're roasting them.	5–8 minutes
Corn	Remove outer husks; gently pull back the green inner husks. Baste with oil or marinade and replace husks. Soak 15–20 minutes and drain.	15–20 minutes
Eggplant	Cut in ½-inch slices or wedges; brush with oil or combination oil/ balsamic vinegar.	8–12 minutes
Endive	Cut in half lengthwise; wash and toss with oil and salt. Grill on cut side only.	10–12 minutes

VEGETABLE	SPECIAL PREPARATION	GRILLING TIME
Fennel	Remove woody root end. Cut horizontally into slices.	15–20 minutes
Leeks	Split lengthwise, rinse well. Trim root ends and tops, leaving 2 inches of green. Cut into 2-inch lengths.	5–6 minutes
Mushrooms	Wash and trim tough stems; grill whole.	10 minutes
Onions	Cut in ½-inch slices or wedges.	10–15 minutes
Potatoes	Cut in ½-inch chunks, uncooked. For small whole potatoes, cook partially.	8–10 minutes 10–15 minutes
Summer squash	Cut lengthwise in ½-inch slices.	8–10 minutes
Tomatoes	Cut into ½-inch slices, or cut in half and roast.	3–4 minutes *(slices)* 10–12 minutes *(halves)*

❋ Roasted Asparagus

Asparagus is one of the first vegetables of the grilling season. Roasting it brings out its natural sweetness. Thicker stalks are better on the grill than thin ones.

I pound asparagus	2 teaspoons lemon juice
I tablespoon olive oil	Salt and freshly ground black
2 teaspoons balsamic vinegar	pepper

1. Preheat a gas grill to medium or use an existing charcoal fire that has burned down to a medium-heat. A grill basket will keep the asparagus from falling through the grill.
2. Cut off the tough ends of the asparagus and, if desired, peel the stalks. In a shallow roasting pan or medium-size cake pan, toss the asparagus with the oil, vinegar, and lemon juice. Season with salt and pepper.
3. Spread out the asparagus evenly in a grilling basket. Close the lid of the grill and roast for 8 to 10 minutes, turning and rolling the spears every few minutes. Test for doneness by piercing with a fork. Sprinkle with additional balsamic vinegar if desired.

MAKES 4 SERVINGS.

✳ Grilled Artichokes
with Cilantro Pesto

Artichokes and cilantro is a taste marriage that begs to be explored.

1 tablespoon lemon juice
¼ to ½ teaspoon salt
3 cloves of garlic, sliced
4 artichokes, bottoms cut flush
and tops of leaves snipped

2 teaspoons olive oil
1 recipe of Cilantro Pesto
(page 151)

1. Combine lemon juice, salt, and garlic in a small stockpot. Add artichokes and simmer in about 2 inches of water for 20 to 30 minutes or until just tender. Set aside or refrigerate for later use.
2. When ready to grill, halve the artichokes and brush with olive oil. Cook on a well-oiled rack over a medium-hot fire for 10 to 12 minutes, grilling cut side first. Flip to heat the outer edges briefly.
3. Serve with Cilantro Pesto or your own favorite dipping sauce.

MAKES 4 SERVINGS, OR 8 APPETIZER-SIZE SERVINGS.

Orange Honey Beets

This recipe will turn the staunchest of beet haters into beet lovers. These taste different than beets cooked any other way.

6 medium-size beets, well scrubbed	1 tablespoon honey
2 tablespoons butter	1 tablespoon orange juice concentrate

1. Boil the beets, whole, in a large saucepan, about 15 to 20 minutes, or cook in a microwave until they are just tender enough to pierce with a fork. Set aside to cool.
2. Preheat a gas grill, build a fire in a kettle grill, or use an existing fire.
3. In a small saucepan, melt butter and add the honey and orange juice.
4. When the beets are cool enough to touch, peel away the coarse outer layer and slice them into rounds, about ⅓ to ½ inch thick. Brush each slice with the honey-orange sauce.
5. Grill beets, turning once, until crisp on the outside yet still soft throughout, about 4 to 6 minutes each side. Brush with the remaining sauce and serve.

MAKES 4 TO 6 SERVINGS.

Grilled Broccoli

Broccoli takes well to the smoky flavor of the grill. Choose your own salad dressing or use a leftover marinade you may have in the refrigerator.

I bunch broccoli
  (about I pound)
⅓ cup bottled salad dressing,
  such as Caesar or shiitake
  mushroom

Freshly ground black pepper

1. Remove the broccoli stems and peel. Quarter lengthwise. Cut the crowns vertically into medium-size florets. Bring a large pot of water to a boil. Add the broccoli and cook, stirring once or twice, until just crisp-tender, 3 to 4 minutes. Drain and rinse under cold water until cool, then pat dry. (This blanching step is optional. It depends on how crunchy you like your broccoli.)

2. In a shallow glass dish, marinate broccoli in the salad dressing for at least 15 minutes. When the grill fire is hot, spread out the broccoli in a vegetable cooking basket, and grill, turning occasionally, until it is lightly browned all over, 6 to 8 minutes.

3. Remove from the grill, season with pepper to taste, and serve hot or warm.

MAKES 4 TO 5 SERVINGS.

Roasted Corn
with Cilantro Butter

It used to be that the sweetness of corn would diminish even 24 hours after picking as the sugars began to turn to starches, but not with today's corn. Newer varieties have more than double the sugar genes. That means they retain their sweetness longer and require only the briefest of cooking. Corn in its husk, cooked on the grill, may take a couple of minutes longer to prepare, but it is definitely one of summer's greatest pleasures.

6 ears fresh corn	1 to 2 cloves garlic, minced
4 tablespoons butter	1/4 teaspoon cumin
1 tablespoon lemon	Pinch of cayenne pepper
or lime juice	Salt
1 1/2 tablespoons minced cilantro	

1. Preheat a gas or kettle grill or use an existing fire.
2. Soak corn in a bucket of cold water for 5 minutes; drain and shake off moisture.
3. In a small saucepan, melt the butter with the lemon or lime juice, cilantro, garlic, cumin, and cayenne. Set aside.
4. Carefully peel back the husks but do not remove them from the ears of corn. Pull off and discard the silk and some of the outer husks. Spread the Cilantro Butter over the corn kernels, dividing it evenly. Pull the husks back up over the kernels and tie in place with a piece of kitchen string or a strip of corn husk.
5. When the fire is hot, lay the ears on an oiled rack. Cover and grill, turning and moving ears frequently, until outside husks are lightly charred

and corn is buttery and tender, about 12 to 15 minutes. Remove the husks and serve.

MAKES 4 TO 6 SERVINGS.

Variation: Corn can also be shucked and wrapped in a single layer of foil and grilled over high heat for 15 to 20 minutes, turning frequently. Try brushing it with Basil Pesto (page 152), lemon juice, and Garlic Oil (page 160), or any leftover marinade.

✻ Grilled Eggplant Slices

This eggplant melts in your mouth. You could top it with a spoonful of Roasted Tomato and Basil Sauce (page 155) or a few gratings of fresh Parmesan cheese.

1 large eggplant (about 1¼ pounds)	2 cloves garlic, minced, or ½ teaspoon garlic powder
3 tablespoons extra-virgin olive oil	½ teaspoon salt
3 tablespoons balsamic vinegar	Freshly grated black pepper

1. Preheat a gas grill to high or build a fire in a kettle grill. Mesquite-flavored chips would taste great but are optional.
2. Slice eggplant crosswise ⅓ to ½ inch thick. In a small bowl, combine the olive oil, balsamic vinegar, garlic, salt, and pepper. Brush both sides of the eggplant slices with this sauce.
3. Place eggplant on the preheated grill. If you wish to have nice grill lines, turn only once on each side. Grill about 10 to 15 minutes. Test for doneness by piercing with a fork.

MAKES 4 TO 6 SERVINGS.

Roasted Eggplant
and Tomato Gratin

1½ pounds ripe tomatoes, sliced ⅓ inch thick

1 pound eggplant, sliced crosswise ⅓ inch thick

2 tablespoons extra-virgin olive oil

½ cup grated Monterey Jack cheese

Salt and freshly ground black pepper

¾ teaspoon chopped fresh sage

¾ teaspoon chopped fresh marjoram

1 to 2 tablespoons freshly grated Parmesan cheese

1. Preheat a gas grill or build a fire in a kettle grill.
2. Lightly brush the tomato and eggplant slices with oil. Arrange the tomato and eggplant slices on the heated grill. Grill, turning once or twice, until the eggplant is golden on both sides and the tomatoes are browned on their edges and softened.
3. Using a spatula, transfer one-third of the tomatoes in an even layer to a 9-inch square baking dish. Cover them with half the eggplant and one-third of the cheese. Repeat. Top with the remaining tomatoes. Season the vegetables with salt and pepper and sprinkle with the herbs. Sprinkle with the remaining Monterey Jack and the Parmesan. Cover with aluminum foil and return to the grill for 20 minutes, or until lightly golden. Set aside for about 15 minutes before serving.

MAKES 4 TO 6 SERVINGS.

❋ Roasted Garlic

Slow-roasted garlic is delectable and so easy to prepare when you already have the grill going. It is surprisingly sweet and mellow. Cloves can be squeezed out and spread on bread or eaten as an accompaniment to polenta or grilled vegetables.

3 to 4 whole heads of garlic	Sprinkle of freshly ground
Drizzle of olive oil	black pepper
2 to 3 tablespoons vegetable	2 sprigs of fresh thyme
broth	

1. Build a fire in a kettle grill or preheat a gas grill.
2. Rub the garlic heads between your hands to remove some of the outer papery skins. Slice ¼ inch off the top of each head of garlic to expose some cloves.
3. Cut a piece of aluminum foil large enough to hold the garlic. Place the heads of garlic in the center of the foil and fold up the edges to form a cup. Drizzle olive oil and vegetable broth over the cloves. Sprinkle with pepper and lay the sprigs of thyme on top. Fold edges of foil to form a secure packet.
4. Place the foil packet near the edge of the grill where heat will be lower. Grill until garlic is very tender and soft to the touch, about 35 to 50 minutes.
5. Give each guest a whole head. Squeeze cloves at the base and the rich mellow cloves will pop out. Serve with fresh bread or as a side dish. It is finger-licking good!

Variation: Use this roasted garlic in dressings and marinades or mix with lemon juice, herbs, and extra-virgin olive oil for a dipping sauce (page 154).

❋ Charcoal-Grilled Leeks

4 large or 8 to 10 small leeks

¼ teaspoon salt

2 tablespoons extra-virgin olive
oil or Garlic Oil (page 160)

2 tablespoons balsamic vinegar

Vegetable oil

Freshly grated black pepper

1. Remove the roots and cut most of the greens off the leeks. Keep their bases intact. Halve them lengthwise and rinse the leeks well by gently opening up the layers.
2. Fill a wide skillet with about 1 inch of water. Bring to a boil and add the salt. Lower the heat, add the leeks, and cover. Simmer for 3 to 5 minutes. Remove from heat and set aside to drain.
3. Combine the olive oil and vinegar in a small bowl. Brush both sides of the leeks with it using a small kitchen brush. Brush the grill with vegetable oil. Lay the leeks on the grill and grill on both sides, turning once to make single grill marks.
4. Remove to a serving plate. Drizzle with any remaining oil and vinegar and freshly grated pepper.

MAKES 4 SERVINGS.

Marji's Marinated
Portobello Mushrooms

Sesame or Teriyaki Marinade (page 143) are both great for marinating portobello mushrooms, but this recipe is easier and delectable.

3 medium-large portobello mushrooms	Salt and freshly ground black pepper
¼ cup Caesar salad dressing or a leftover marinade	

1. Preheat a gas grill or build a fire in a kettle grill.
2. Wash mushrooms and remove tough stems. Place mushrooms in a shallow bowl and pour salad dressing or marinade over them. Marinate 15 to 20 minutes, turning occasionally.
3. Grill mushrooms about 6 to 8 minutes per side or until softened and evenly charred. Season with salt and pepper. Cut each one into 1-inch-thick slices and serve.

MAKES 4 SERVINGS.

❦ Grilled Tomatoes
with Red Onion and Basil

Firmer varieties of tomatoes such as Roma or Early Girl will grill best in this recipe. Add 1 or 2 yellow tomatoes for a radiantly colored dish (yellow tomatoes tend to grill more quickly).

1 tablespoon extra-virgin olive oil	½ cup chopped fresh basil
1 tablespoon balsamic vinegar	Salt and freshly ground black pepper
4 to 5 medium-size tomatoes, sliced ½ inch thick	Freshly grated Parmesan cheese or thinly sliced fresh mozzarella (optional)
1 medium-size red onion, sliced ½ inch thick	

1. Preheat a gas grill to medium-high or use an existing charcoal fire. It is most convenient to place tomatoes on the grill after other foods have been cooked, as they tend to be messy (but definitely worth it).
2. Add the olive oil and balsamic vinegar to a small bowl. Brush the sliced tomatoes and onion with it. Carefully place them on the grill, turning only once for perfect grill lines. The tomatoes will cook much faster than the onions.
3. Remove the tomatoes from the grill and layer them in a square baking dish that can be used on the grill. When onions have cooled enough to touch, break them into rings and layer them over the tomatoes. Top with chopped basil, salt, and pepper. Sprinkle with additional olive oil and balsamic vinegar if desired. Top with thin slices of fresh mozzarella or freshly grated Parmesan. Cover with aluminum foil and return the pan to the grill for an additional 4 to 5 minutes or until cheeses are melted.

MAKES 4 SERVINGS.

❋ Marinated and Grilled Summer Squash

Crookneck, yellow, zucchini, and the round yellow sunburst squash all come to life on the grill.

1 pound small summer squash, yellow or crookneck	¾ cup Teriyaki Marinade (page 143) or Herb Vinaigrette (page 145)

1. Preheat a gas grill to high or build a fire in a kettle grill.
2. Wash squashes and slice lengthwise into quarters or slices about ⅓ inch thick.
3. Place marinade in a shallow bowl. Add squash to the bowl and marinate 30 to 60 minutes, turning occasionally.
4. Place squashes in a vegetable grilling basket and grill 8 to 10 minutes, turning, until squashes are charred but still fork-tender.

MAKES 4 TO 6 SERVINGS.

Kabobs

Kabobs are one of the most festive and fun foods to cook on the grill. In order to have successful kabobs, where all the foods are cooked but not overcooked, it is best to choose foods that cook in the same amount of time. Pictures in books show colorful kabobs filled with a variety of foods, but I prefer to thread only two or three kinds of food on a kabob—using ones that will cook for about the same amount of time. Tomatoes and mushrooms do well together; tofu, fresh pineapple, and seitan are good. Peppers and onions cook in about the same amount of time. Some foods are best precooked before they are added to the kabob: potatoes and carrots, for example.

If you make kabobs this way, they can be passed to each person or served on a platter so each person can take as much as desired.

Wooden skewers should be soaked for 30 minutes before going on the grill so they won't burn. Quality metal skewers have notches so that food won't twist on the skewer every time you turn it on the grill; these are worth the extra cost.

Summer Vegetable Kabobs
with Seitan

1 8-ounce package of seitan,
rinsed and cut into 1-inch
cubes (well-drained, firm
tofu would also work well)

2 bell peppers, a variety of
colors, cut into 1½-inch
pieces

2 to 3 small summer squash,
cut ¾ inch thick

½ of a fresh pineapple, cut in
chunks or 8-ounce can of
pineapple chunks

1 recipe of Herb Marinade
(page 144)

2 to 3 small boiling onions
or 1 medium-size red onion,
quartered and layers
separated

½ pound mushrooms, rinsed

2 to 3 firm Roma tomatoes,
quartered

Vegetable oil

1. Place seitan, all cut–up vegetables, and pineapple in a large plastic container with a tight-fitting lid. Add the marinade and marinate in refrigerator for 6 to 12 hours. While they marinate, turn the container upside down or stir every few hours so marinade soaks through all vegetables.
2. Preheat a gas grill to medium-high or build a fire in a kettle grill.
3. Using metal skewers, thread several skewers with seitan, peppers, and onion. Make several other skewers with pineapple, mushrooms, squash, and tomatoes. Each of these groups will grill about the same amount of time.
4. When grill is hot, brush with oil. Grill, turning occasionally, for 8 to 12 minutes. Place skewers on a large platter so that each person can take as much of each one as they want.

MAKES 6 TO 8 SERVINGS.

Vegetable Kabobs
with Lemon Curry Marinade

2 tablespoons canola oil

1 medium-size onion, minced

3 cloves garlic, minced

½ teaspoon each: ground ginger, salt, turmeric, chili powder, and ground cumin

¼ teaspoon freshly ground black pepper

¼ teaspoon dry mustard

Juice of 1 lemon

2 tablespoons tomato paste

6 tablespoons plain low-fat yogurt

¼ cup low-fat sour cream

2 tablespoons water

1 red pepper, seeded and cut into 1-inch chunks

2 small zucchini, sliced into ⅓-inch rounds

16 small mushrooms, cleaned

2 yellow squash, sliced into ⅓-inch rounds

6 small onions, peeled and quartered

Vegetable oil

1. To prepare the marinade, heat oil in a medium-size skillet and sauté the onion and garlic for 3 to 4 minutes or until onions are translucent. Add the ginger, salt, turmeric, chili powder, cumin, pepper, and dry mustard; sauté for an additional 3 to 4 minutes on medium-low heat. Remove from heat and stir in the lemon juice, tomato paste, yogurt, sour cream, and water. Use a blender if desired.

2. Add the cut-up vegetables to a wide, shallow bowl. Add the cooled curry mixture and marinate for at least 4 hours in the refrigerator. Arrange the vegetables on skewers, alternating ingredients. The remaining sauce may be used to baste while grilling and as a dipping sauce at the table.

3. When grill is hot, brush with oil. Grill the kabobs over medium-high heat for approximately 10 to 15 minutes, turning every few minutes. Test with a fork; vegetables should be charred and fork-tender. Serve hot or at room temperature.

MAKES 4 TO 6 SERVINGS.

Other Vegetable Dishes

Ragout of Summer Vegetables with Tarragon

This colorful side dish features the subtle flavor of tarragon. It's best made in a skillet on top of the stove where the flavorful juices will not be lost.

2 tablespoons butter

1 cup sliced white onion

2 cloves garlic, minced

1 cup chopped sweet yellow pepper

1 cup chopped sweet red bell pepper

3 small zucchini, cut in half lengthwise and sliced

2 cups sliced mushrooms

2 tablespoons lemon juice

2 tablespoons chopped fresh tarragon or 2 to 3 teaspoons dried

Salt and freshly ground black pepper to taste

1. In a large skillet with a lid, sauté onions and garlic in butter for 2 to 3 minutes or until onions turn translucent. Add peppers and sauté another 3 to 4 minutes. Add the zucchini, mushrooms, and lemon juice, cover, and simmer 4 to 5 minutes or until vegetables are just crisp-tender.
2. Remove the lid, stir in the tarragon and sprinkle with salt and pepper. Simmer 1 to 2 minutes longer to allow herb flavor to blend.

MAKES 4 SERVINGS.

Grilled Vegetables
with Goat Cheese Herb Sauce

This simple but elegant dish can be served on a large platter with bowls of dipping sauce for each guest. With no marinade on the vegetables, their simple smoky flavors are very distinct.

3 medium-size bell peppers (a variety of colors), quartered lengthwise

2 medium-size zucchini, sliced lengthwise ⅓ inch thick

3 small yellow squash, sliced lengthwise ⅓ inch thick

1 medium-size red onion, cut crosswise into 4 slices

1 small eggplant, sliced in ⅓-inch rounds

4 small tomatoes, cut cross-wise into thick slices

2 tablespoons extra-virgin olive oil

Salt and freshly ground black pepper

2 tablespoons minced fresh basil

2 teaspoons minced fresh oregano

1 teaspoon minced fresh tarragon

⅔ cup low-fat milk

2 cloves garlic, minced

3 to 3½ ounces mild goat cheese, fontina, or other good melting cheese

1. Preheat a gas grill or light a hot fire in a kettle grill.
2. Brush the cut sides of all the vegetables with a small amount of olive oil. Season with salt and pepper.
3. Grill the peppers, skin side down, for about 12 minutes, or until charred. Grill the zucchini, yellow squash, and onion, turning once or

twice, until tender—about 5 to 7 minutes. Grill the eggplant 8 to 10 minutes, turning once. Grill the tomatoes, turning once, about 5 minutes or until slightly softened.

4. Place peppers in a tightly closed plastic bag until cool. Remove the skin and cut peppers into large strips. Arrange all the grilled vegetables on a platter or large plates. Sprinkle with 2 tablespoons of the fresh herbs and keep warm in a low oven.

5. In a small saucepan, bring the milk, the remaining herbs, and garlic to a simmer over low heat for 3 to 5 minutes. Whisk in the goat cheese until it is melted and sauce is smooth. Sprinkle with pepper.

MAKES 4 TO 6 SERVINGS.

Serving Suggestions: Serve the goat cheese sauce in bowls for dipping, accompanied by a bowl of Gazpacho Rose soup (see page 177) and a warm loaf of grilled bread. This is vegetarian ecstasy!

Variation: This dish is also great served with Mustard Crème Fraîche Sauce (page 157), Cilantro Pesto (page 151), Basil Pesto (page 152), or Avocado Aioli (page 153).

4/27/04 excellent

❋ Grilled Vegetable Ratatouille

For best flavor, prepare this recipe about an hour before guests arrive. Ratatouille never tasted so good as when it is infused with the smoky flavor of the grill.

2 tablespoons extra-virgin olive oil

1 medium-large eggplant, sliced ⅓ inch crosswise

1 large red onion, sliced ⅓ inch thick

1 red bell pepper, halved, seeded

1 yellow bell pepper, halved, seeded

1 green bell pepper, halved, seeded

3 medium-size tomatoes, cut bite-size

3 tablespoons chopped fresh basil

3 tablespoons balsamic vinegar

2 tablespoons capers

Salt and freshly ground black pepper

¼ cup chopped Italian parsley

1. Brush all vegetables except the tomato with olive oil and grill until fork-tender. Set aside to cool.
2. Place cut-up tomatoes in a large bowl. Add the basil, vinegar, capers, salt, pepper, and parsley. When the grilled vegetables have cooled enough to touch, peel peppers and dice all vegetables into uniform bite-size pieces. Add to the bowl and toss to mix.
3. Set aside for 30 minutes or up to 2 hours to allow flavors to marry. Serve warm or at room temperature.

MAKES 6 TO 8 SERVINGS.

6. Mix the couscous and pesto sauce together. Add more pesto to taste. Fill the well of each tomato with the couscous and pesto combination. Top with a sprinkling of Parmesan. Return the tomatoes to the grill, well side up. You may want to place them in an aluminum foil cake pan or use a 9-by-9-inch cake pan that is reserved for grill use. Grill until the cheese is golden in color and tomatoes are soft but not mushy. Top with a sprig of parsley or basil leaf.

MAKES 6 TO 8 SERVINGS.

Roasted Red, White, and Blue Black Casserole

1 large eggplant
1 medium-large onion,
  sliced ½ inch thick
2 to 3 tablespoons olive oil
3 large vine-ripened tomatoes

½ cup chopped fresh basil
  or 2 teaspoons dry basil
6 ounces mozzarella cheese
Salt and freshly ground black
pepper

1. Preheat a gas grill to medium-high or prepare a fire in a kettle grill.
2. Remove the cap and blossom ends of the eggplant. Quarter the eggplant lengthwise, then slice each quarter again into ⅓-inch slices lengthwise. Brush eggplant and onion with olive oil.
3. When the grill is hot, grill each slice of eggplant about 5 to 6 minutes on each side or until lightly charred and softened. Grill onions until lightly charred. Set aside.
4. Cut tomatoes in half and slice thinly. Slice the cheese. Pull onions apart to make onion rings.
5. With the remaining olive oil, oil a 9-by-6-inch baking dish (2-quart). Spread half the onions on the bottom and sprinkle with half the basil. Starting at one end of the dish, arrange alternate standing layers of one slice of eggplant (skin side up), 2 slices of tomato, and then a slice of cheese. Repeat this pattern, working down the baking dish. When all the tomato, eggplant, and cheese have been fitted in, top with the remaining basil and onions. Sprinkle with salt and pepper and cover the dish tightly with aluminum foil.

6. Arrange the coals in the kettle grill for indirect heating or turn one burner off on the gas grill. Place the baking dish on the burner that is turned off. On a kettle type grill, wait until the coals have cooled somewhat to a medium-high heat. Roast, covered, on the grill for 25 to 40 minutes or until eggplant is completely softened and cheese is melted.

MAKES 6 TO 8 SERVINGS.

Roasted Herbs
and Vegetables

By creating a good indirect source of heat, you can use the grill for slow roasting. These roasted vegetables will fill the air with the redolence of rosemary, garlic, and thyme.

2 large Spanish onions
or 8 small onions (about
1½ inches in diameter)
4 large carrots
or 12 whole baby carrots
8 to 10 small potatoes (red or
white thin-skinned potatoes)
1 green or red pepper, cut into
medium-size squares
2 tablespoons olive oil

1 tablespoon butter
4 to 5 garlic cloves, minced
2 tablespoons lemon juice
1 tablespoon minced fresh
rosemary or 1 teaspoon dry
2 teaspoons minced fresh
thyme or ½ teaspoon dry
Salt and freshly ground black
pepper to taste

1. Prepare the grill for indirect heat by following instructions in chapter 2.
2. Peel all the vegetables. If using large onions, cut each one into eighths by slicing it lengthwise into quarters and then cutting each quarter crosswise. If using large carrots, halve them lengthwise and cut into 2-inch sections. Quarter the potatoes.
3. Place all vegetables in a large salad bowl. In a small saucepan, melt olive oil and butter. Add garlic, lemon juice, and herbs. Pour over vegetables and toss with your hands.
4. Arrange all vegetables in a large baking dish. Cover tightly with aluminum foil and place on the grill for 35 minutes. Reserve any remaining olive oil and sauce that may be at the bottom of the bowl for later use.

5. Uncover and turn the vegetables with a large spoon. Add salt and pepper and brush with remaining olive oil. Roast, uncovered, for another 15 to 20 minutes or until the edges of vegetables have browned and are fork-tender.
6. Remove from the oven and arrange vegetables on a platter. Serve hot or at room temperature.

MAKES 6 TO 8 SERVINGS.

✿ Roasted Roots

As summer moves into the cool evenings of fall, rediscover your roots—root vegetables, that is! Slow roasting gives them an entirely different quality and taste, reminiscent of your mother's Sunday pot roast. This dish could be baked in an oven at about 350 degrees, but it also does great on a medium-hot grill.

2 large carrots	1 head garlic
2 medium-size parsnips, about ½ pound	3 tablespoons extra-virgin olive oil
1 large leek	¾ teaspoon salt
2 small young turnips, about ¼ pound	¾ teaspoon freshly ground black pepper
4 small new potatoes, about ½ pound	5 fresh thyme sprigs, each 5 inches long
2 medium-size shallots	4 fresh rosemary sprigs, each 5 inches long
1 medium-size red onion	

1. Make a fire in a kettle grill or preheat a gas grill to medium-high. Prepare the grill for indirect heat by following instructions in chapter 2.
2. Wash all vegetables. With a vegetable peeler or paring knife, peel the carrots and parsnips. Cut the carrots into 2-inch lengths. Cut the parsnips in half crosswise, separating the tapering root end from the thick upper portion. Cut the upper portion lengthwise into 2 to 4 pieces, depending on thickness. Cut off all but ½ inch of the greens from the leek and reserve for another use. Cut the remaining white portion of leek into 2 pieces. Cut away any leaves from the turnips, leaving a ½-inch stub. Trim off any imperfections from the potatoes but do not peel. If using

larger potatoes, halve or quarter them. Peel the shallots, but do not cut off the root ends as they help the shallots to retain their shape during cooking. Peel the red onion and quarter it lengthwise. Separate the garlic head into cloves; peel the cloves but leave them whole.

3. Combine the olive oil, salt, pepper, thyme, and rosemary sprigs in a 9-by-9-inch square baking pan or disposable aluminum foil pan. Add all of the vegetables and toss with your hands until they are well coated with the herbs and oil. Cover pan with foil.

4. Place the pan of vegetables on the grill and roast for 20 to 25 minutes. Turn the roots and brush with some of the reserved olive oil mixture. Remove the foil and continue roasting, turning once or twice and basting with more olive oil, if desired, until all of the vegetables are tender and are easily pierced with a fork, about 10 to 15 minutes more.

5. Remove from the grill and arrange the roots on a serving platter. Serve hot or at room temperature with Mustard Crème Fraîche Sauce (page 157) and accompanied by a salad of mixed greens and crusty bread.

MAKES 4 TO 6 SERVINGS.

Corn-Stuffed Bell Peppers

This dish makes a colorful centerpiece for a meal.

5 medium-size red or green bell peppers

1 medium-size onion

1 tablespoon butter

2 to 3 cloves garlic, chopped or minced

2 cups fresh or frozen corn kernels

2 tablespoons seeded fresh or canned jalapeño chilies

2 tablespoons finely diced cilantro

1¼ cups grated sharp cheddar cheese

1. Preheat a gas grill to medium-high or build a fire in a kettle grill.
2. Cut off stem ends of peppers and remove seeds. Leave 4 of the peppers whole. Finely chop the remaining bell pepper and the onion.
3. Melt butter in a large frying pan over medium-high heat. Add the chopped pepper, onion, and garlic, stirring often, until onion is soft (about 7 to 10 minutes). Add corn kernels, jalapeño, and cilantro to the pan and cook, stirring, until corn is hot. Place in a bowl and set aside.
4. Place whole peppers on the grill for about 5 to 7 minutes total, turning them every couple of minutes until they are lightly charred but not overly softened. (You could do this in your oven at 400 degrees for about 10 minutes.).
5. Add cheese to the corn and mix lightly. When peppers have cooled, cut in half and fill each one with the corn mixture.
6. Set peppers, filling side up, on a lightly greased grill over medium-hot coals. Cover the grill and cook until pepper shells are soft and cheese is melted, about 10 minutes. You may want to place them on a pizza warming tray.

MAKES 4 SERVINGS, OR 8 APPETIZER-SIZE SERVINGS.

7 ✳ CHAPTER

Salad Dressings, Salsas, Side Dishes, Spreads, and Sauces
(Marinades and Pickles, Too!)

A BEAUTIFUL SUNNY DAY AND FRIENDS AROUND THE GRILL ARE the first ingredients for great grilled food, but it is the sauces, marinades, and side dishes that turn good food into a memorable meal.

Marinades are one of the most useful methods for adding interest and character to foods, especially those that are to be grilled. The basic components of a liquid marinade are an acid, seasonings, and an oil. The acids most commonly used are mellow flavored vinegars, lemon juice, wine, or tomatoes. Seasonings consist of fresh or dried herbs, garlic, soy sauce, and hot or sweet peppers. Olive oil or a dark-flavored sesame oil are the primary oils used in the marinades and dressings that follow.

The oil plays an important role in the process of grilling vegetables as it helps prevent the cut sides from drying out on the fire. (If the vegetables have been coated with a marinade, there is no need to brush them with oil.) Because the marinades in this book are not used on meats, they can be returned to the refrigerator to be reused or made into a salad dressing. (It is not safe to reuse a marinade in which raw meat or seafood has soaked.)

Smoky, hot foods from the grill are accented nicely with the bold flavors and texture of salsas. Not just for scooping up onto chips anymore, salsas make a lively accompaniment to a variety of grilled foods. With a little imagination you can create your own.

A good salsa is made with colorful combinations of fresh, ripe produce, interesting textures, and a balance of flavors such as hot and spicy, acidic and sweet. Roma tomatoes work best in tomato salsas because they are firmer and less watery than other tomatoes.

This chapter also contains a variety of sauces for dipping, side dishes that will help round out a menu, and various condiments.

Salad
Dressings
and
Marinades

❋ Sesame Marinade

This marinade is perfect for tofu. If you really want tofu to absorb the flavor, it needs to marinate a minimum of 12 hours in the refrigerator. I have often left it for 24 hours, which is even better—it just takes planning ahead.

½ cup soy sauce

¼ cup lemon juice

½ cup rice vinegar

¼ cup Asian-style sesame oil

1 tablespoon hot chili
    sesame oil

2 teaspoons grated fresh ginger

3 cloves garlic, minced
    or pressed

Freshly ground black pepper

Combine all ingredients and blend well.

MAKES ABOUT 1½ CUPS.

Note: Hot chili sesame oil is found in the international section of the supermarket (Chinese foods).

Teriyaki Sauce
or Marinade

This sauce tastes much fresher and doesn't overpower like some commercial teriyaki sauces. It will keep in the refrigerator for 2 to 3 weeks, or cut this recipe in half. This marinade can also be reduced by boiling (uncovered) until it becomes a syrup for a more robust taste.

½ cup dry sherry
2 tablespoons grated
  fresh ginger
2 garlic cloves
  Freshly grated black pepper

½ cup soy sauce
2 tablespoons packed light
  brown sugar
2 tablespoons rice wine vinegar

In a blender or small food processor, combine ingredients. Blend until smooth.

MAKES ABOUT 1¼ CUPS.

Herb Marinade

½ cup balsamic vinegar
¼ cup extra-virgin olive oil
2 tablespoons water
4 cloves garlic, minced
½ cup chopped fresh basil
2 tablespoons minced fresh
   rosemary

1 tablespoon minced fresh
   oregano
1 tablespoon honey
   or brown sugar
Salt and freshly ground black
   pepper

Blend all ingredients in a blender or food processor. In a glass bowl, pour marinade over vegetables.

MAKES 1 CUP.

❋ Herb Vinaigrette

1 large clove garlic, peeled
⅛ teaspoon salt
2 tablespoons balsamic vinegar
2 tablespoons white wine vinegar
2 tablespoons lemon juice
2 tablespoons water

1 teaspoon Dijon-style mustard
3 tablespoons olive oil
1 tablespoon fresh oregano
 leaves
2 teaspoons fresh thyme leaves

Add all ingredients to the blender. Blend until smooth. Refrigerate until needed.

MAKES ABOUT ¾ CUP.

Tomato Basil Salad Dressing

This simple summer salad dressing uses ripe tomatoes to replace some of the oil usually found in dressings.

2 Roma tomatoes
or 1 large tomato

3 cloves garlic

2 tablespoons extra-virgin olive oil

2 tablespoons water

2 tablespoons balsamic or white wine vinegar

8 to 10 large leaves of fresh basil (to taste)

¼ teaspoon salt

1 tablespoon freshly grated Parmesan cheese

Freshly ground black pepper and a pinch of cayenne

Place all ingredients in a blender or food processor. Blend until smooth.

MAKES ¾ CUP.

Low-Fat Ranch Dressing

⅓ cup reduced-fat mayonnaise
1 cup buttermilk
2 tablespoons chopped chives
   or green onions (tops only)
3 to 4 sprigs fresh parsley

¾ teaspoon garlic powder
¾ teaspoon onion powder
   Pinch of cayenne pepper,
   paprika, salt, and black
   pepper

Combine all ingredients in a blender or food processor. Puree until smooth. Refrigerate 1 hour to allow flavors to blend.

MAKES 1½ CUPS.

❈ Eileen's Salad Dressing or Marinade

This delicious salad dressing contains brewer's yeast, which is a great source of B-complex vitamins.

⅓ cup good-quality vegetable oil
¼ cup red or white wine vinegar
½ a medium-size onion, sliced

2 tablespoons soy sauce
4 tablespoons nutritional yeast

Place all ingredients in a blender or food processor. Blend until smooth. This can be stored in the refrigerator for up to 10 days.

MAKES ABOUT I CUP.

Sauces

Barbecue Sauce

This barbecue sauce will keep in the refrigerator for up to three weeks and has an unmatched piquant flavor. Most commercial barbecue sauces are too heavy-tasting for use with tofu or other vegetable dishes.

1 medium-size onion, finely diced	2 teaspoons salt
2 cloves garlic, chopped	1 teaspoon allspice
2½ cups tomato sauce	½ teaspoon cayenne pepper (or to taste)
¼ cup water	2 tablespoons chopped parsley
½ cup honey	¾ cup lemon juice
2 tablespoons molasses	1 tablespoon soy sauce
⅓ to ½ cup grainy mustard	½ teaspoon liquid smoke

Combine all ingredients in a medium-large saucepan. Bring to a boil; reduce heat and simmer for 1 hour. When sauce has cooled slightly, place in a blender to puree.

MAKES ABOUT 3½ CUPS.

❋ Cilantro Pesto

This pesto is delicious as a dipping sauce for grilled vegetables. Or surprise your family by using it as a topping for pasta.

2 tablespoons shelled
pistachio nuts
¼ cup water
2 tablespoons olive oil

½ teaspoon sea salt
2 cloves garlic
1 cup cilantro leaves

Place all ingredients in a blender. Blend until smooth and creamy.

MAKES ABOUT ¾ CUP.

Basil Pesto

Summer without pesto is like spring without daffodils. There are probably about as many pesto recipes as there are avid cooks. This one is a starting-off place, so add to it according to your own tastes.

½ cup basil leaves

5 tablespoons extra-virgin olive oil

2 tablespoons freshly grated Parmesan cheese

3 tablespoons chopped walnuts or pine nuts

3 to 5 cloves garlic (more if you like)

2 tablespoons parsley

1 tablespoon water (optional)

1 tablespoon lemon juice

Salt

Combine all ingredients in a blender or food processor. Blend until smooth but not pureed. Taste and adjust seasoning.

MAKES ABOUT ¾ CUP.

❋ Avocado Aioli

Aioli is the Provençal name for a garlicky mayonnaise often served with a tray of vegetables for dipping. Serve this Avocado Aioli with a platter of roasted or grilled vegetables or as a dipping sauce for kabobs.

2 ripe Hass avocados
(about ½ pound each)
2 tablespoons fresh lime juice
2 tablespoons extra-virgin
olive oil

2 to 3 cloves garlic, minced
¼ cup finely chopped cilantro
Salt and freshly ground black
pepper

1. Halve the avocados and scoop the flesh into the bowl of a food processor. Add the lime juice, olive oil, and garlic. Puree.
2. Scrape the puree into a bowl and fold in the cilantro. Season with salt and pepper. Refrigerate up to 2 hours before serving.

MAKES ABOUT 1½ CUPS.

❈ Roasted Garlic Paste

½ cup extra-virgin olive oil
1 head of roasted garlic, cloves
separated and peel removed

1 to 2 tablespoons lemon juice
Salt and freshly ground black
pepper

Place olive oil, garlic cloves, and lemon juice in a food processor or blender. Blend until smooth. Add salt and pepper to taste.

MAKES ABOUT ½ CUP.

Serving Suggestions: Spread on bread or use to make a sauce for grilled vegetables.

❋ Roasted Tomato and Basil Sauce

Smoke-scented tomatoes make a versatile sauce. When the coals are starting to die down and we are ready to sit down to dinner, I often put a few ripe tomatoes on the grill to roast slowly (brushed with oil, as tomatoes tend to stick). I roast them until they are browning and oozing juices. The peels come off easily once they have cooled. I make a sauce by pureeing them with a little salt, olive oil, and balsamic vinegar. Refrigerate for later, or use them as a delicious sauce over pasta or on toasted bread.

6 to 8 ripe medium-size tomatoes, roasted and peeled

I small onion, roasted and diced

10 to 12 large basil leaves, finely chopped

3 to 4 cloves garlic, minced

2 tablespoons extra-virgin olive oil

Pinch of salt and freshly ground black pepper

Mash the roasted, peeled tomatoes with a potato masher. Place tomatoes in a small saucepan, add all other ingredients, and simmer for 5 minutes, until warmed through and flavors have deepened.

MAKES I CUP.

Crème Fraîche

This lightened version of traditional Crème Fraîche is useful to have in the refrigerator to top potato dishes, tortilla and bean dishes, or a bowl of berries. Substitute a low-fat sour cream or a mixture of sour cream and yogurt if you don't have some on hand.

1 pint half-and-half	⅓ cup buttermilk

Combine ingredients in a quart-size glass jar. Swirl them around to mix. Cover, and leave jar on a countertop for 24 hours at room temperature. Shake occasionally. Sometimes this takes a little longer to set, but I return it to the refrigerator after a day even if it hasn't quite gelled. (It will set in the refrigerator.)

MAKES ABOUT 2½ CUPS.

Mustard Crème Fraîche Sauce

This sauce is great with grilled vegetables or kabobs and wonderful with salmon.

1 tablespoon grated zest of lemon	¼ teaspoon salt
1 tablespoon lemon juice	½ cup Crème Fraîche (page 156),
2 tablespoons grainy, flavorful mustard	or substitute low-fat sour cream and/or plain yogurt

In a bowl, whisk the lemon zest, lemon juice, mustard, salt, and Crème Fraîche together. Use warm to baste food or as a sauce.

MAKES ABOUT ⅔ CUP.

Honey Yogurt Sauce

This low-fat sauce is a perfect alternative to ice cream when you need a dollop of something to top a dessert.

1 cup nonfat yogurt	2 tablespoons honey
1 cup low-fat sour cream	1 teaspoon vanilla

Combine all ingredients in a medium-size bowl. Stir with a spoon.

MAKES ABOUT 2 CUPS.

Spreads and Dips

❈ Garlic Oil

I use this all the time to brush on grilled vegetables, bread, or in place of olive oil in marinades.

| 10 to 12 cloves garlic | 1 cup extra-virgin olive oil |

1. Crush garlic cloves with the side of a French knife and remove papery skin. (A French knife has an arched blade and is an essential tool for chopping and mincing vegetables as well as many other uses.) Put garlic in a clean glass jar and pour in olive oil; cover with a lid or cork.
2. Let oil and garlic stand at room temperature for at least 48 hours before use. Then keep refrigerated between uses.

MAKES ABOUT 1 CUP.

Garbanzo Spread

This simple spread is nutritious and delicious. Use it on crackers or as a filling for pita bread pockets with fresh vegetables.

1 15-ounce can garbanzo beans (low-sodium variety)	4 green onions, finely chopped
2 to 3 cloves garlic	2 tablespoons finely chopped parsley
1 to 2 tablespoons mayonnaise or low-fat yogurt	½ 3.5-ounce can chopped olives
1 tablespoon lemon juice	Freshly grated black pepper
⅛ teaspoon salt	

1. Drain garbanzo beans and rinse. Add them to a food processor along with the garlic, mayonnaise, lemon juice, and salt. If using a blender, more liquid may be needed, such as a tablespoon of water.
2. Remove to a serving bowl and add the green onions, parsley, and chopped olives. Top with freshly grated black pepper.

MAKES 4 TO 6 SERVINGS.

❋ Olive Tapenade

This Olive Tapenade can be used on warm French bread, brushed on vegetables, or Roasted Potatoes Wedges (page 75).

⅔ cup medium-size pitted
ripe olives
2 tablespoons pine nuts
2 tablespoons water
2 teaspoons capers

2 to 3 garlic cloves
1 to 2 tablespoons extra-virgin
olive oil
Salt and freshly ground black
pepper

Place all ingredients in a blender or food processor and blend until smooth.

MAKES 1 CUP.

Roasted Red Pepper Dip

Use this dip for a tray of raw or grilled vegetables, or spread it on crackers or French bread.

1 large red bell pepper (about 10 ounces)	2 tablespoons mayonnaise
1 to 2 cloves garlic	⅛ teaspoon white pepper
¼ cup nonfat yogurt	Salt (optional)

1. Preheat a gas grill to high or build a fire in a kettle grill (or use an existing fire).
2. Cut pepper in half and remove seeds and core. Place pepper on the grill until charred on all sides, turning as needed—about 10 to 12 minutes. Place pepper in a sealed plastic bag until cool; then remove skin with fingers.
3. In a blender or food processor, puree pepper, garlic, yogurt, mayonnaise, and white pepper. Add salt if desired. Refrigerate for later use or serve at room temperature.

MAKES 1 CUP.

Salsas and Side Dishes

Before serving a salsa, let it stand for 15 to 20 minutes to allow the flavors to deepen. Salsas are best served at room temperature or slightly chilled. Most salsas are best eaten within a few hours of being made.

❋ Black Bean Salsa

2 cups black beans, cooked,
   or 2 15-ounce cans, drained
1 fresh jalapeño pepper, diced
¼ cup *each* diced red and
   yellow bell pepper
3 to 4 green onions, sliced

2 tablespoons chopped cilantro
1 to 2 cloves garlic, crushed
¼ cup diced tomato
3 tablespoons olive oil
2 limes (juice and zest)
   Salt and pepper to taste

Mix all ingredients. If the jalapeño is too hot for your taste, remove its seeds or use a little less of its flesh. Let flavors blend for 1 to 2 hours.

MAKES 3½ CUPS.

❋ Grilled Corn
and Avocado Salsa

This salsa/side dish is perfect with grilled vegetables, salmon, tomato soup, or any Mexican entrée.

3 ears corn, husked	1½ tablespoons chopped fresh
1 tablespoon extra-virgin	cilantro or ½ teaspoon
olive oil	cumin
1 large tomato	¼ teaspoon salt
1 to 2 jalapeño peppers	⅛ teaspoon freshly ground
2 cloves garlic, minced	black pepper
2 tablespoons lime juice	½ avocado

1. Prepare a hot fire in the grill. We like our corn just grilled. If you prefer a more cooked taste to your corn, precook it for 2 minutes in boiling water. Drain and cool.
2. Brush corn with olive oil. Grill, turning occasionally, until it has light brown grill marks evenly distributed. Cut tomato in half and grill, turning once, until skin is slightly charred and tomato is softened, about 3 to 5 minutes. Place whole jalapeños on the grill, turning frequently, until skin is charred, about 5 to 7 minutes.
3. While the grilled vegetables are cooling, combine garlic, lime juice, cilantro, salt, and pepper in a medium-size bowl. Peel avocado and cut into ½-inch pieces; add to the bowl. Cut corn kernels off cob and add to the bowl. Peel tomatoes (skin will come off easily) and jalapeños. For a milder flavored salsa, remove the seeds from the jalapeño pepper. Chop tomatoes and jalapeños finely and add to the bowl. Toss to mix and serve at room temperature.

MAKES 5 TO 8 SERVINGS.

❋ Cucumber, Avocado, and Red Pepper Salsa

This fresh vegetable combination makes a great salsa or accompaniment for any rice dish, vegetable kabobs, or a summer soup.

½ of a medium-size cucumber, seeded and diced

1 small red pepper, diced

¼ cup finely sliced green onions or chives

1 small jalapeño pepper, cored, seeded, and finely chopped

1 tablespoon chopped cilantro

1 tablespoon fresh lime juice

1 to 2 tablespoons rice vinegar

½ teaspoon salt (or more to taste)

Freshly ground black pepper

1 medium-size avocado, peeled and diced

In a small bowl, combine all ingredients except avocado. Gently toss in the avocado and set aside for 20 minutes before serving.

MAKES ABOUT 2 CUPS.

White Bean Relish

This bean relish makes a great side dish to add protein to a simple meal.

1 16-ounce can navy beans, drained and rinsed
1 cup finely chopped tomato
¾ cup sliced green onion
½ cup finely chopped celery
¾ cup finely chopped sweet red pepper
2 tablespoons chopped fresh cilantro

2 tablespoons chopped parsley
1 jalapeño pepper, seeded and chopped
1 envelope Italian dressing mix
1 clove garlic, minced
½ cup water
¼ cup white wine vinegar
1 to 2 tablespoons olive oil

1. Combine first 8 ingredients in a medium-size bowl; set aside.
2. Combine dressing mix and remaining ingredients in a jar. Cover tightly and shake vigorously. Pour dressing over relish mixture and toss gently. Cover and refrigerate for at least 2 hours. Toss again before serving. Serve relish with a slotted spoon.

MAKES 6 TO 8 SERVINGS.

Ketchup
and Relishes

Most of us think of condiments as those convenient items that live on the shelves of our refrigerator door. In this chapter you will find a few that you can make yourself. They are easy to prepare, and their fresh flavors are in another dimension from those commercially available.

Your Own Tomato Ketchup

Make your own ketchup? Sure you can! I found this recipe in Sharon Cadwallader's column in the *San Francisco Chronicle*. I cut it in half to make it easier to try.

4 pounds ripe tomatoes, cored and quartered	1½ cups sugar or ¾ cup honey
1 pound apples, cored and quartered	1½ tablespoons salt
3 large onions, peeled and chopped	1 teaspoon cloves
1½ cups distilled white vinegar	½ teaspoon freshly ground black pepper
	¾ teaspoon allspice

1. Place all ingredients in an 8- to 10-quart stockpot. Bring to a boil, reduce heat and simmer, uncovered, for 3 hours, stirring frequently.
2. Strain mixture through a sieve or cool it enough to put it through a food processor. Reheat to boiling and pour into sterilized jars and seal. Turn jars upside down for 10 minutes to help lids seal.

MAKES 4 TO 5 PINTS.

Easy Refrigerator Dill Pickles

Your own pickles? Yes, you can make them too! These pickles do not require canning. The recipe yields enough to enjoy for a couple of weeks as well as some to give away. If pickling cukes are not available at your grocery store, try the local farmers' market.

2 pounds pickling cucumbers (about 15 medium-size)

2 cups water

1½ cups white distilled vinegar

2 tablespoons whole pickling mix

2 cloves garlic, peeled and halved

10 to 12 whole peppercorns

5 heads fresh dill (tops only) or 1 tablespoon dried dill

1½ teaspoons salt

1. Scrub cucumbers with a vegetable brush. If using cukes larger than 4 inches long, slice, quarter, or halve lengthwise. Place all cut-up cucumbers in a large glass or ceramic salad bowl (do not use wood or metal). Add the water, vinegar, pickling mix, garlic, peppercorns, dill, and salt to the bowl. Stir gently to mix.
2. Cover the bowl with a plate or plastic wrap. Let sit unrefrigerated for 12 to 24 hours; then place bowl in the refrigerator. Pickles are ready to eat after 24 to 36 hours. After three or four days, I often pour off some of the brine and dilute it with water so that the pickles do not continue to get stronger in flavor. Pickles will keep in the refrigerator for up to 3 weeks.

MAKES ABOUT 3 QUARTS.

Adelle's Sweet Tomato Relish

This tomato relish is one of our all-time favorite summer treats. It is a specialty of my neighbor, Adelle Charlson, who is ninety-three years old. She taught home economics for over thirty years and is one of the best cooks I know.

24 ripe tomatoes	¼ cup celery seeds
2 onions	3 to 4 cups sugar
2 green peppers and 2 red peppers (or use all green)	4 cups white distilled vinegar
¼ cup mustard seeds	2 tablespoons salt

1. Using a food chopper or food processor, grind the tomatoes, onions, and peppers. Drain this through a strainer lined with cheesecloth. Reserve the juice for drinking.
2. Pour the tomato mixture into an 8- or 10-quart stockpot. Add the mustard seeds, celery seeds, sugar, vinegar, and salt. Boil for 20 minutes. Pour into sterilized jars and seal.

MAKES ABOUT 4 PINTS.

Summer Soups

MENTION SOUPS AND MOST PEOPLE CONJURE UP IMAGES OF A frosty winter evening and a cozy fire, but soups can have their place in a summer menu as well. They bring a certain zing and thirst-quenching quality to summer brunches, picnics, and barbecues. Most are uncooked and are simple to prepare. Best of all, soups are full of garden-fresh vegetables and, yes, fruits too. A summer soup can be used as an appetizer, the main attraction, or a simple but elegant dessert.

Summer soups are often served chilled. With a few exceptions, they taste best when removed from the refrigerator about 20 minutes before serving. Extra seasonings may be required in a soup that is served cold.

We eat with our eyes as well as our mouths, so the right garnish may make the difference between rave reviews and upturned noses. A garnish, especially on a pureed soup, provides some variety in texture as well as an eye-appealing color change. It can be as simple as a dollop of sour cream or yogurt, chopped scallions, a few toasted nuts, crumbled bacon, or a leaf of a fresh herb.

Soup is one of the most comforting and satisfying foods—not just for winter nourishment, but to offset the hot summer doldrums, too.

Cold Soups

Great Gazpacho

Summer without gazpacho is unthinkable. This sweet-and-sour flavored recipe is easy to prepare in a blender or food processor.

2 tablespoons lemon juice	1 cucumber, peeled, seeded,
1 tablespoon sugar	and diced
¼ cup red wine vinegar	1 green pepper, seeded and
½ teaspoon salt	chopped
2 tablespoons olive oil	2 cups diced tomatoes
2 cloves garlic	3 stalks celery, finely chopped
3 to 4 large tomatoes,	1 carrot, grated
quartered (to equal about	6 green onions, finely sliced
2½ cups juice)	½ cup chopped fresh basil

1. Place the first seven ingredients in a blender or food processor and puree. Transfer to a large serving bowl and add the cucumber, green pepper, diced tomatoes, celery, carrot, green onions, and basil.
2. Chill thoroughly. Remove from the refrigerator 20 minutes before serving.

MAKES 8 TO 10 FIRST-COURSE SERVINGS.

Gazpacho Rose

Children sometimes balk at all the vegetables in the previous recipe. For some mysterious reason, this simple pureed version of gazpacho is always a hit with them. Juicy, vine-ripened red tomatoes, either from your garden or a local farmers' market, are a must.

6 ripe tomatoes, quartered
⅓ cup lightly packed fresh basil leaves
2 cloves garlic, peeled
Salt and freshly ground black pepper to taste

1 cup good-quality buttermilk or plain low-fat yogurt
Sugar or lemon juice (optional)
Garnish: Sliced scallions or basil leaves

1. In a food processor or blender, puree the tomatoes, basil, garlic, salt, and pepper until smooth. Stir in the buttermilk and taste for seasoning. Add a touch of sugar or a few drops of lemon juice if you feel it needs it.
2. Chill and serve in iced cups. Garnish with scallions or basil leaves.

MAKES 4 TO 6 SERVINGS.

Watermelon Soup

While the guests wait for those coals to be just right at the next family barbecue, surprise them by serving a thirst-quenching Watermelon Soup. A
seedless watermelon is the perfect choice for it. If you don't have one, a
good food processor will puree the seeds (and they're good for you too!).

6 cups cold watermelon juice
(about 3 pounds
watermelon)
1¾ cups buttermilk
or plain yogurt

½ teaspoon rosewater
(optional)
Pinch of salt
Garnish: Chilled watermelon
balls or a sprig of mint

Process watermelon in a food processor or blender until you have 6 cups
juice. Add the buttermilk, rosewater, and salt and blend. Chill for at least
2 hours. Garnish with watermelon balls and/or a sprig of fresh mint.

MAKES 6 TO 8 FIRST-COURSE SERVINGS.

Berry Soup
with a Sparkle

Most berries have about a three-week season, so have your recipe ready. This summer dessert is elegant and simple to prepare.

6 cups ripe berries, stemmed and washed (use strawberries, raspberries, blackberries, or an assortment)

1 cup orange juice

3 tablespoons freshly squeezed lemon juice

½ cup sugar or 2 to 3 tablespoons honey (blackberries may need more sweetening)

2 cups sparkling water

1 quart vanilla ice cream or frozen yogurt

Garnish: Whole fresh berries

1. Combine the berries and citrus juices in a blender or food processor and puree until smooth. Work in batches, if necessary.
2. Transfer to a serving bowl and stir in the sugar and sparkling water. (If you use honey, add it to the blender with berries.) Cover and refrigerate until chilled, at least 2 hours.
3. Ladle into chilled bowls, top with a small scoop of ice cream or frozen yogurt, and garnish with whole berries.

MAKES 6 TO 8 FIRST-COURSE SERVINGS.

Variation: For an extra-special evening, substitute 2 cups champagne or other sparkling wine for the sparkling water.

Corn and Dill Chowder

When corn is still abundant but the enthusiasm for another evening of corn on the cob is waning, use fresh sweet corn for this easy summer soup.

2 cups cooked corn kernels
1 bunch scallions
or 5 to 6 green onions
(including 2 inches of green),
sliced
Juice of ½ lime or lemon
2 teaspoons fresh dill
leaves

¼ teaspoon salt
Freshly ground black pepper
1 quart buttermilk
or plain yogurt
Garnish: Fresh dill sprigs

1. In a blender or food processor, puree the corn, scallions, lime or lemon juice, dill leaves, salt, and pepper until smooth. Add 1 cup of the buttermilk and process until blended. Transfer the mixture to a serving bowl and whisk in the remaining buttermilk.
2. If serving cold, chill in the refrigerator for at least 1 hour and garnish with a small dill sprig. This soup can also be heated gently before serving.

MAKES 4 TO 6 SERVINGS.

Warm Soups

Light and Easy Zucchini Soup

With most soups it takes a day to allow the flavors to marry, but this one tastes great when made at the last minute (even better the next day). Fresh herbs are the secret to great taste. If you use dried herbs, be sure they haven't been in the cupboard for more than six months, as they lose their potency.

2 pounds small zucchini

½ cup minced shallots
   or a combination of shallots
   and onions

2 tablespoons butter

6 cups well-flavored vegetable
   broth or 4 cups chicken
   stock plus 2 cups water

1½ teaspoons white wine vinegar

¼ cup quick-cooking Cream
   of Wheat

1½ tablespoons fresh dill
   or tarragon, or 2 teaspoons
   dry herb

¼ teaspoon salt

½ teaspoon white pepper

⅛ teaspoon black pepper

1 cup light sour cream
   or a mixture of sour cream
   and nonfat yogurt

Garnish: Fresh dill

1. Trim the zucchini and cut into half-inch chunks; reserve.
2. In a small stockpot, cook the shallots in the butter for several minutes until tender but not browned. Add the zucchini chunks, broth, and vinegar. Bring to a boil, then stir in the Cream of Wheat. Simmer, partially covered, for 15 to 20 minutes. Season with dill or tarragon, salt, and white and black pepper. Puree and return the soup to the pan.
3. Bring the soup to a simmer just before serving and beat in ½ cup of the sour cream. Ladle the soup into bowls, place a dollop of sour cream on each portion, and garnish with fresh herb.

MAKES 4 TO 6 SERVINGS, OR UP TO 10 FIRST-COURSE SERVINGS.

Kamp Bell's
Creamy Tomato Soup

This soup could be called Tomato Soup, 1950s Retro. It was a foundation food in our diets when we were kids. We floated as many Saltine crackers in the bowl as would fit. You can make this out of fresh tomatoes from the farmers' market or sweet, heavy, ripe ones from your own garden.

2 tablespoons olive oil	⅛ teaspoon freshly ground
1 medium-size onion, chopped	black pepper
2 pounds ripe red tomatoes,	¼ teaspoon white pepper
quartered or 1 28-ounce	1 cup milk
can stewed tomatoes	2 to 3 teaspoons balsamic
2 cups well-flavored vegetable	vinegar
stock	Garnish: ¼ cup thinly sliced
3 sprigs fresh basil	fresh basil
¾ teaspoon salt	

1. In a large soup pot, heat the olive oil over medium-high heat. Add the onion and cook, stirring occasionally, until softened, about 5 minutes. Add the tomatoes, stock, basil, salt, and pepper to the onions. Bring to a boil over high heat, reduce the heat to medium-low and simmer, uncovered, until reduced by one-quarter—about 25 minutes. Remove the basil sprigs.

2. Cool slightly. Puree the soup in batches in a blender until very smooth. Return to the pot and bring to a simmer over medium heat. Stir in the milk and balsamic vinegar. Adjust seasonings—you may want to add ½ teaspoon sugar if tomatoes are not at their peak of ripeness, or additional balsamic vinegar. Cut the basil leaves very thinly just before serving. Ladle the hot soup into bowls and garnish with basil.

MAKES ABOUT 4 CUPS OR 6 SERVINGS.

Mediterranean
Shepherd's Soup

The shepherds on the hills around the Mediterranean would boil water with lots of garlic, a few tomatoes, and sprigs of the wild herbs that grew around them. This is a much more elegant version of their simple fare—perhaps my all-time favorite soup. It's perfect for early fall when tomatoes are still plentiful.

5 tablespoons olive oil	1 4-inch sprig of fresh rosemary
2 large onions, chopped	or ½ teaspoon dried
10 cloves garlic, peeled	2 to 3 leaves fresh sage
4 to 5 medium-size very ripe	or ½ teaspoon dried
tomatoes or 2½ to 3 cups	Salt and freshly ground black
stewed tomatoes	pepper to taste
5 cups well-flavored vegetable	8 thick slices of French bread
stock or water	(white or whole-wheat)
2 long sprigs of fresh thyme	4 to 6 ounces freshly grated
or ½ teaspoon dried	Parmesan or Gruyère cheese

1. In a 10-inch skillet, heat 3 tablespoons of the olive oil over medium heat. Add the onions and sauté until softened, about 5 minutes. Lower the heat slightly, put 4 cloves of garlic through a garlic press, and add them to the pan. Sauté 2 more minutes, stirring almost constantly. Add the tomatoes and stir-fry for 1 minute.
2. Pour the sautéed vegetables into a large soup pot. Deglaze the skillet with a little of the stock or water and add the pan contents and remainder of the liquid to the soup pot. Add the herbs, salt, and pepper. Bring to a boil, then cook at a low simmer, uncovered, for about 20 minutes.

3. Preheat the oven to 400 degrees or use an existing fire in the grill.
4. Mince 3 of the remaining garlic cloves in a garlic press and add to the remaining 2 tablespoons of olive oil; mix well. Brush each slice of French bread on one side with this oil. Divide the grated cheese among the bread slices, piling it onto the garlicky side of each one, pressing the cheese down slightly with your finger. Place the cheese-covered bread on a baking sheet or on the grill (using a pizza warming tray on the grill makes them very easy to handle). Grill until bubbly, about 4 to 5 minutes.
5. Mince the remaining 3 cloves of garlic in the garlic press and add directly to the soup. Let the soup simmer another 5 minutes. Place one grilled slice of bread in the center of each soup bowl and ladle the hot garlic soup over it. Pass additional grated cheese around the table if you desire.

MAKES 6 SERVINGS AS AN ENTRÉE, OR 8 TO 10 FIRST-COURSE SERVINGS.

Soup on
the Grill

❄ Roasted Garlic
and Red Pepper Soup

This soup begins on the grill as the garlic and red peppers are roasted. Then the other ingredients are added and finished on the stove. Its smoky, rich flavor is balanced nicely with a dollop of Crème Fraîche or yogurt.

1 whole head of garlic	½ teaspoon salt (or to taste)
1 to 2 tablespoons olive oil	½ teaspoon white pepper
3 to 4 large red bell peppers	(or to taste)
1 large yellow onion, sliced	2 tablespoons sherry
2 stalks celery, sliced	Pinch cayenne
5 cups well-flavored vegetable	Garnish: Light sour cream,
stock	Crème Fraîche (page 156),
¾ teaspoon fresh thyme	plain yogurt (optional), or
or oregano	minced chives

1. Preheat a gas grill to high or build a fire in a kettle grill. Brush grill lightly with a good-quality vegetable oil.
2. Slice just the tops of the garlic cloves off a head of garlic. Peel off some of the loose outer skin. Place whole head of garlic on a piece of aluminum foil that is large enough to wrap it firmly, but leave it slightly open at the top. Pour a little olive oil over garlic bulb and a tablespoon of vegetable broth or water. Place packet on the outer edge of the grill or where you know the heat is less intense. Roast until garlic is light brown and bubbly—about 25 to 40 minutes. When it has cooled sufficiently to touch, squeeze the garlic out of each clove. Set aside.
3. Cut peppers in half, remove seeds and membranes, and place on the

grill. Close the lid and roast peppers, cut side down, 3 to 4 minutes. Turn peppers and repeat process until they become evenly blackened— about 8 to 12 minutes. Remove pepper from the grill and place in a plastic bag to steam. When cool, peel off skin and set aside.

4. In an 8- to 10-quart stockpot, sauté onion and celery in olive oil until lightly caramelized. Add the stock and simmer, covered, for about 20 minutes. Add the roasted peppers and garlic, thyme, salt, and pepper. Cook an additional 15 minutes. Puree this mixture in a food processor or use a hand-held mixer. Add the sherry and cayenne and bring to a boil, being careful not to scald the bottom of the pan. Garnish with a generous dollop of sour cream or plain yogurt. Crusty bread is a good accompaniment.

MAKES 6 SERVINGS.

❈ Grilled Vegetable Soup

This is the perfect soup for that first cool evening of September when the garden is still overflowing with vegetables. Double the recipe to freeze some for a convenient meal on a busy winter evening.

2 tablespoons olive oil

I small eggplant, sliced lengthwise ½ inch thick

I medium zucchini, sliced lengthwise ½ inch thick

2 medium-size yellow squashes, sliced lengthwise ½ inch thick

I medium-size red onion, cut crosswise into 4 slices

I medium-size bell pepper (red, yellow, or green), halved lengthwise

3 garlic cloves, minced

2 pounds ripe tomatoes, coarsely chopped

4 cups well-flavored vegetable or chicken stock

Salt and freshly ground black pepper

3 tablespoons finely chopped fresh basil (about 10 to 12 leaves)

1½ teaspoons finely chopped fresh oregano (optional)

Garnish: Sliced basil leaves or spoonful of freshly grated Parmesan cheese (optional)

1. Preheat a gas grill to high or build a fire in a kettle grill. Brush the grill lightly with olive oil or other vegetable oil.

2. Brush the eggplant and the cut sides of the zucchini and yellow squash with olive oil. Grill the eggplant, squashes, and onion, turning occasionally, until tender but still firm: approximately 6 to 8 minutes for the squashes and onion and 8 to 10 minutes for the eggplant. Grill the pepper cut side down for 3 to 4 minutes and the skin side down until evenly

charred all over—about 8 to 10 minutes. Place pepper in a plastic bag until cool enough to touch; then peel off the skin.

3. Heat 2 teaspoons olive oil in a large saucepan or small stockpot. Add the garlic and stir over moderate heat. Add the tomatoes, stock, salt, and pepper and simmer, covered, for 10 minutes.

4. While stock simmers, cut up all the grilled vegetables into ½-inch dice. Add to the pan along with the basil and oregano. Simmer, stirring, for 3 minutes longer. Garnish the soup with a slice of basil leaf or a small spoonful of fresh Parmesan. Bruschetta from the grill or a slice of crusty bread are perfect partners.

MAKES 8 TO 10 SERVINGS.

9 ✳ CHAPTER

Summer Salads

EVERYONE LOVES THE CRISP, FRESH TASTE OF SALADS. BECAUSE most can be prepared ahead of time, they are a great convenience when entertaining.

Salads have come a long way. Gone are the days when a salad meant iceberg lettuce, a little tomato, a slice of cucumber, and a glop of fatty dressing on top. Today's salads are grilled or tossed, grain- or fruit-based, and contain a myriad multihued greens.

Many of the salads in this chapter are dynamic enough to be the main attraction—especially in summer when lighter and simpler meals are called for. Just add bruschetta, cornbread, a slice of frittata, or warmed tortillas and you have a meal.

Main-Dish
Salads

Taco Salad

This family-pleasing salad is a meal in itself. Serve it with warmed tortillas or Skillet Cornbread with Jalapeños (page 102).

1½ cups cooked brown or white
    long-grain rice
1 tablespoon margarine
    or butter
½ medium-size onion, minced
¾ teaspoon chili powder
⅛ teaspoon coriander
½ teaspoon cumin powder
2 cloves garlic, minced
⅛ teaspoon cayenne
¼ teaspoon salt (optional)
1 15-ounce can kidney beans,
    rinsed and drained

1 small head iceberg lettuce,
    cut into bite-size pieces
1 3.5-ounce can fire roasted
    chilies
1 4-ounce can sliced pitted
    black olives
3 tomatoes, diced
¼ pound cheddar cheese,
    grated
Salsa (optional)
¼ pound baked tortilla chips,
    broken into bite-size pieces

1. Prepare rice ahead of time or use leftover rice.
2. In a medium-size skillet, sauté the butter, onion, cooked rice, chili powder, coriander, cumin, garlic, cayenne, and salt for 4 to 5 minutes. Allow to cool and transfer to a large bowl. Add to this the kidney beans, lettuce, canned chilies, olives, tomatoes, and grated cheese.
3. Mix in about ¼ cup of Low-Fat Ranch Dressing (page 147) and 2 to 3 tablespoons salsa. Crumble tortilla chips into salad just before serving.

MAKES 6 TO 8 SERVINGS.

❋ Mediterranean Salad with Lentils

⅓ cup sun-dried tomatoes
(not packed in oil)

1 cup uncooked lentils

1 teaspoon fresh thyme
or ¼ teaspoon dried

3 cloves garlic, minced

2 bay leaves

4 cups water

¾ cup chopped red or yellow
sweet pepper

¾ cup chopped celery

¼ cup finely chopped onion

¼ cup finely chopped parsley

3 tablespoons red wine vinegar

2 tablespoons olive oil

1 teaspoon Dijon-style mustard

1 teaspoon crushed fennel
seeds

¼ teaspoon salt

¼ teaspoon freshly ground
black pepper

4 cups salad greens, washed
and dried

1. Place dried tomatoes in a bowl and cover with boiling water; set aside.
2. Rinse lentils. Bring lentils, thyme, garlic, bay leaves, and 4 cups water to a boil in a medium-size saucepan Reduce heat, cover, and simmer about 25 to 35 minutes or until lentils are tender, stirring occasionally.
3. Combine sweet pepper, celery, onion, and parsley in a large salad bowl. Combine vinegar, oil, mustard, fennel, salt, and pepper in a separate small bowl; stir until smooth.
4. When dried tomatoes are soft, drain, chop, and add to vegetables.
5. Drain lentils, discarding bay leaves. Toss lentils with vegetables and dressing. Line four plates with salad greens. Divide lentil mixture among plates and serve immediately; or cover lentil mixture and chill.

MAKES 4 SERVINGS.

✳ Chinese Chicken-less Salad

1 small head Napa cabbage, shredded	2 cloves garlic, minced
¼ head red cabbage, shredded	2 tablespoons sesame oil
1 bunch green onions, sliced	6 tablespoons white wine vinegar
3 tablespoons finely chopped cilantro	3 tablespoons sugar
½ cup chopped almonds	2 3-ounce packages of Ramen
½ cup sesame seeds	noodles, crushed; include
1 tablespoon soy sauce	spice packets in salad

1. Combine the cabbages, green onions, and cilantro in a large salad bowl. In a small sauté pan, toast the chopped almonds. Remove nuts from pan and add to the salad bowl. Using the same pan, toast the sesame seeds, then add them to the salad bowl.

2. Add the soy sauce, garlic, sesame oil, vinegar, and sugar to the sauté pan and warm through until dissolved. Add this to the salad bowl along with the spice packets from the Ramen noodles. Add the crushed Ramen noodles to the salad and serve.

MAKES 6 SERVINGS.

Variation: Place the almonds and sesame seeds in the center of a square of heavy-duty aluminum foil. Drizzle 1 to 2 teaspoons peanut or other vegetable oil over the nuts and toss to coat. Fold up edges of foil, pinching together to make a secure packet. Place the packet on the coolest part of the grill, shaking several times until toasted, about 5 to 7 minutes.

Caponata

Serve this traditional Italian appetizer over grilled polenta for a hearty main dish.

1 medium-size unpeeled eggplant, cut in ¾-inch cubes	3 large tomatoes, seeded and diced
Salt	1 cup water
Nonstick vegetable cooking spray	1 tablespoon capers
2 cups diced celery	¼ cup sliced pimento-stuffed olives
3 tablespoons extra-virgin olive oil	2 tablespoons sliced ripe olives, drained
1 large onion, chopped	3 tablespoons minced parsley
3 tablespoons wine vinegar	Freshly ground black pepper to taste
1 teaspoon sugar	

1. Place eggplant cubes in a colander and salt them lightly. Allow to sit for 15 to 20 minutes while you chop other vegetables. Coat an 8- or 10-quart Dutch oven with nonstick cooking spray. Sauté celery in 1 tablespoon olive oil, stirring occasionally, until soft. Remove and set aside.

2. Rinse the eggplant in the colander to remove salt; pat dry. Add the remaining 2 tablespoons of oil, eggplant, and onion to the Dutch oven and cook, stirring, until eggplant is fork-tender and onions are soft, about 8 to 10 minutes. Remove eggplant and onion and set aside with the celery.

3. Add the vinegar, sugar, tomatoes, and water to the same pan; cook, stirring occasionally, for 5 minutes.

4. Return vegetables to pan. Stir in the capers, olives, and parsley. Reduce heat and simmer, uncovered, until about half the liquid evaporates (about 10 minutes). Add salt and pepper to taste, if desired. Cool, cover, and chill until next day or for as long as 5 days. Bring to room temperature before serving.

MAKES 8 SERVINGS.

❋ Quinoa and Pecan Salad with Dried Cranberries

This salad is made with quinoa, a recently reintroduced grain. It has a zesty combination of textures and flavors.

3½ cups water
1½ cups quinoa
1 bunch green onions,
  finely sliced
½ cup diced dried cranberries
¾ cup finely diced celery
⅓ cup finely chopped flat-leaf
  parsley
¾ cup coarsely chopped pecans

2 tablespoons extra-virgin
  olive oil
¼ cup lemon juice
2 tablespoons rice wine vinegar
1 tablespoon sesame oil
½ teaspoon salt
⅛ teaspoon freshly ground
  black pepper
Pinch of cayenne pepper

1. Bring water to a boil. Add quinoa, stir, cover, and reduce heat to a simmer. Cook until quinoa is soft, about 20 minutes.
2. Add green onions, dried cranberries, celery, and parsley to a large salad bowl. Toast the pecans in a small skillet and add to the salad bowl. Add the olive oil, lemon juice, vinegar, sesame oil, salt, and peppers to the bowl. Stir to mix.
3. Stir in the quinoa when it has cooked and cooled slightly. Set aside for an hour if possible; serve at room temperature.

MAKES 8 TO 10 SERVINGS.

Green Salads

Warm Spinach and Basil Salad

This salad makes a nice accompaniment to soup or a first course before pasta.

4 cups fresh spinach leaves

2 cups inner leaves romaine lettuce

1 cup chopped fresh basil

3 tablespoons extra-virgin olive oil

3 cloves garlic, minced

½ cup pine nuts, toasted

2 tablespoons white wine vinegar

2 tablespoons lemon juice

Salt and freshly ground black pepper to taste

½ cup freshly grated Parmesan cheese

1. Wash and dry the spinach, romaine, and basil. Chop or tear apart leaves and toss together in a large salad bowl.
2. Heat the oil in a small skillet over medium heat. Add the garlic and pine nuts and sauté until the nuts begin to brown slightly. Add vinegar and lemon juice just to warm. Season to taste with salt and pepper.
3. Toss the spinach, romaine, and basil with the warm dressing and Parmesan. Serve immediately.

MAKES 4 MAIN-COURSE SERVINGS, OR 6 TO 8 FIRST-COURSE SERVINGS.

Mushroom, Blue Cheese, and Walnut Salad

This simple salad is a staple at our house. It never fails to get recipe requests every time I serve it.

2 tablespoons extra-virgin olive oil

¼ cup fresh chopped basil or 2 teaspoons dry

½ teaspoon salt

⅛ teaspoon freshly ground black pepper

⅛ teaspoon paprika

2 teaspoons Dijon mustard

2 to 3 tablespoons white wine vinegar

½ pound mushrooms, sliced

1 bunch green onions, thinly sliced

5 cups bite-size pieces of romaine

½ cup walnut pieces

3 ounces blue cheese, crumbled

About 10 cherry tomatoes or 2 large tomatoes, cut up

1. In a large salad bowl, combine oil, basil, salt, pepper, paprika, mustard, and vinegar. Beat with a fork until blended. Mix in mushrooms and green onions; let stand at room temperature to marinate while preparing the remaining ingredients.

2. Add cut-up romaine to the salad bowl. Add walnut pieces, blue cheese, and tomatoes to the salad bowl and toss lightly. (To crumble blue cheese more easily, place in the freezer for 10 minutes first.)

MAKES 4 TO 6 SERVINGS.

Green Bean Salad
with Yogurt Dill Dressing

Serve this flavorful salad when the garden is overflowing with green beans or there's a great buy at the market.

¾ cup water

1½ pounds green beans,
  ends trimmed

1 3.5-ounce can pitted, sliced
  black olives, drained

2 large firm-ripe tomatoes,
  cut into wedges

½ cup chopped walnuts

½ cup plain nonfat yogurt

2 tablespoons extra-virgin
  olive oil

¼ cup finely chopped fresh dill
  or 2 tablespoons dry

2 tablespoons lemon juice

2 cloves garlic, minced

¾ teaspoon white pepper

¼ teaspoon salt

Garnish: Dill sprigs

1. In a 5- to 6-quart pan, bring about ¾ cup water to a boil over high heat. Add beans and reduce heat; simmer, covered, just until beans are tender to bite, about 5 minutes. Drain and immerse beans in ice water. When cool, cut diagonally into 3-inch lengths.

2. In a large salad bowl, combine beans, olives, tomatoes, and walnuts.

3. In a separate bowl, combine yogurt, olive oil, dill, lemon juice, garlic, white pepper, and salt. Add to the salad bowl and stir to combine. Garnish with dill sprigs.

MAKES 6 TO 8 SERVINGS.

Grilled
Salads

❋Bulgur and Black Bean Salad with Grilled Corn and Chilies

A couple cups of mesquite chips on the grill really bring out the flavor of the chilies and corn in this hearty dish.

2 to 3 Anaheim chilies (or Poblano chilies for a more piquant taste)

1 ear of corn, shucked and washed

1 tomato, sliced in half crosswise

1¾ cups water

1 cup bulgur

½ teaspoon salt

1 15-ounce can black beans, rinsed and drained

6 to 7 sliced green onions

2 tablespoons chopped cilantro

3 tablespoons olive oil

3 tablespoons white wine vinegar

Freshly ground black pepper

Garnish: Avocado slices and/or salsa

1. Light a fire in a charcoal grill or preheat a gas grill to medium-high.
2. When the fire is hot, lay the chilies, corn, and tomato on the rack. Cover and grill, turning occasionally. Leave corn on the grill until light charred marks are evenly distributed. Remove tomato when it is softened and lightly charred on the edges. Set them aside to cool. Leave the chilies on the grill until they are charred all over—about 8 minutes. Place the hot chilies in a plastic bag to steam until they are cool enough to touch.
3. In a medium-size saucepan, bring 1¾ cups of water to a boil. Add the bulgur and salt, cover, reduce the heat to low, and cook until the bulgur has absorbed all the water. This will take only about 5 minutes. Remove from the heat and let stand, covered, while preparing the vegetables.

4. Remove the corn from the cob. Rub away the burned skin of the chilies and chop finely. Dice the tomato. Add all these vegetables to a large salad bowl. Add the bulgur, beans, green onions, cilantro, olive oil, and vinegar. Season with a generous grinding of black pepper. Toss all ingredients and set aside for 30 minutes. Serve at room temperature. Garnish with a slice of avocado and/or a spoonful of salsa.

MAKES ABOUT 6 SERVINGS.

❦ Moroccan Couscous Salad with Grilled Peppers

This salad is best if you let it stand at room temperature for at least 1 hour or up to 4 hours before serving.

2 medium-size bell peppers (a mix of colors)

2½ cups water

1½ cups couscous

½ teaspoon salt

3 tablespoons extra-virgin olive oil

¼ cup fresh lemon juice

1 teaspoon ground cumin

Freshly ground black pepper

2 cloves garlic, minced

Pinch of cayenne pepper

1 pound ripe tomatoes, seeded and cut into ½-inch dice

1 large seedless cucumber, peeled and cut into ½-inch dice

½ cup coarsely chopped, pitted Kalamata olives

5 to 6 green onions, minced

3 tablespoons finely chopped flat-leaf parsley

1. Roast the bell peppers over a medium-high flame, turning, until charred all over. Transfer the peppers to a plastic bag and let steam until cool enough to handle. Remove the blackened skin, cores, and seeds. Cut the peppers into ½-inch dice.

2. In a saucepan, bring 2½ cups water to a boil. Stir in the couscous and ½ teaspoon salt. Turn down the flame, cover, and simmer for 2 to 4 minutes. (Don't leave the stove, as couscous will be finished cooking before you can finish any other task.) Remove from the heat and let stand. In a small bowl, combine the olive oil, lemon juice, cumin, black pepper, garlic, and cayenne.

3. Fluff the couscous with a fork and add to a large salad bowl. Add the roasted peppers, tomatoes, cucumber, olives, and green onion. Pour the dressing over the couscous and toss to combine. Just before serving, stir in the parsley.

MAKES 8 TO 10 SERVINGS.

❋ Grilled Corn, Pepper, and Tomato Salad

Tired of corn on the cob? This colorful grilled salad combines nicely with a variety of dishes and keeps well in the refrigerator for up to two days.

5 ears of corn	¼ cup dry white wine
1 sweet green pepper	¼ cup lemon juice
1 small red onion	2 to 3 large cloves garlic,
2 tomatoes, diced	minced
1 bunch green onions, sliced	1 tablespoon minced fresh
¼ cup finely chopped parsley	thyme or 1 teaspoon dried
¼ cup finely chopped fresh basil	Salt and freshly ground black
2 tablespoons extra-virgin	pepper to taste
olive oil	

1. Build a fire in a kettle grill or preheat a gas grill to high.
2. While the grill is heating, wash and shuck the corn. If you prefer a more cooked texture or if the corn is a few days old, precook it for 3 to 4 minutes on the top of the stove. Cut bell pepper in half and remove inner core. Cut ½-inch thick slices of red onion.
3. Combine diced tomatoes, green onions, parsley, and basil in a large salad bowl and set aside.
4. Lightly brush the corn and onion with a small amount of olive oil. Grill at high temperature until corn has an even distribution of brown grill marks and peppers are evenly charred. Grill onion until brown on the edges and softened.

5. While grilled vegetables are cooling, heat the remaining olive oil, wine, lemon juice, garlic, thyme, salt, and pepper in a small saucepan. Cook for 3 to 4 minutes. Add to the salad bowl when it has cooled slightly.
6. Cut corn kernels from the cobs and dice red onion and green pepper. Add to the salad bowl and adjust seasonings. Refrigerate or serve at room temperature.

MAKES 6 TO 8 SERVINGS.

❦ Roasted Pepper and Tomato Salad

This Mediterranean-inspired roasted pepper salad is easy to make on the grill. It needs time to allow the flavors to marry, so plan to make it early in the morning and serve later. It is an excellent appetizer, but in hot summer weather it makes a full meal, accompanied by crusty bread, cheese, and a glass of ice tea or chilled wine.

6 large bell peppers (a variety of colors)	1 teaspoon cumin
5 medium-size garden-ripened tomatoes (about 2½ pounds)	4 cloves garlic, minced or pressed
15 pitted black olives	1 tablespoon white wine vinegar
2 tablespoons extra-virgin olive oil	3 tablespoons chopped parsley
½ teaspoon salt	Lettuce leaves
⅛ teaspoon freshly ground black pepper	Garnish: Parsley sprigs or Parmesan cheese shavings (optional)

1. Light a hot fire in a charcoal grill or preheat a gas grill to high.
2. Wash and cut peppers in half, removing the seeds and inner membrane. When the fire is hot, place peppers on the rack. Cover and grill, turning them occasionally, until they are evenly charred all over, about 8 to 10 minutes. Place peppers in a plastic bag and close tightly. Allow peppers to "sweat" for 10 to 15 minutes to loosen the skins. Remove skins by pulling with your fingers. Cut peppers into strips, about ½ inch by 1 inch.
3. Add peppers to a large salad bowl; cut tomatoes into ½-inch pieces and add to bowl. Slice olives in half and add.

4. Combine oil, salt, pepper, cumin, garlic, vinegar, and parsley in a small bowl; stir to blend. Add to the pepper mixture.
5. Cover salad and let stand at room temperature for at least 2 hours, or refrigerate for as long as 2 days. Bring to room temperature before serving.
6. To serve, line individual plates with lettuce leaves and mound pepper mixture onto lettuce. Garnish with additional sprigs of parsley or a few shavings of fresh Parmesan.

MAKES 6 TO 8 SERVINGS.

❋ Grilled Portobello Mushroom and Asparagus Salad

One could live on this salad for a great many days and not tire of it. Portobellos on the grill—it's a perfect marriage.

2 ounces (about 3 cups) leaf lettuce
2 ounces (about 3 cups) mesclun-type mix of young greens
1 medium-size shallot
1 teaspoon Dijon mustard
3 tablespoons sherry wine vinegar
1 tablespoon lemon juice

1 teaspoon fresh thyme leaves
4 tablespoons extra-virgin olive oil
Pinch of salt and freshly ground black pepper
1 pound portobello mushrooms, stems removed
1 pound thick asparagus, woody ends removed
Vegetable oil to brush on grill

1. Preheat a gas grill to medium-high or build a fire in a kettle grill.
2. Wash, dry, and tear up lettuces. Place in a large salad bowl and set aside.
3. Place the shallot, mustard, vinegar, lemon juice, and thyme in a blender; blend until smooth. With the machine running, add 3 tablespoons oil in a slow, steady stream. Season with salt and pepper to taste.
4. Brush the mushrooms and asparagus with remaining olive oil and sprinkle with salt and pepper. Brush the grill lightly with vegetable oil. Put the mushrooms on the grill, turning occasionally to avoid sticking. Add the asparagus and grill, rolling spears frequently to avoid burning. Grill the mushrooms about 10 to 14 minutes total. They should be crispy at the edges but still juicy. Cook the asparagus until browned and

crisp-tender, about 6 to 8 minutes, depending on their thickness. Remove from the grill and set aside to cool.

5. Drizzle the salad dressing over the greens and toss well. Cut the asparagus and the mushrooms into 1-inch lengths. Add to the salad and mix in with the lettuces.

MAKES ABOUT 6 SERVINGS.

10 ❋ CHAPTER

Desserts

THE PROCESSION OF RIPENING FRUIT THROUGHOUT SUMMER IS like a symphony with different instruments being added to and subtracted from the music. During the dark rainy days of March I long for the taste of strawberries and rhubarb. Just as I've had my fill, cherries, apricots, and raspberries become available. Blueberry season arrives almost immediately after that. When the peaches, melons, and nectarines ripen, a full orchestra of tastes and pleasures emerges. Naturally ripened fruit adds a richness to one's culinary summer experience like nothing else.

Years ago I lived in an orchard in the Santa Cruz mountains and all my favorite fruits were right outside the back door. When I moved to my new home, I immediately started scouting out the best sources for good fruit: I found a U-pick at the edge of the suburbs; generous neighbors with too many fruit trees (and perhaps an interest in something I could trade); and a fruit stand along my husband's commute route.

With the increasing popularity of farmers' markets, naturally ripened fruit (and vegetables) are within the reach of more consumers. Organic produce is also becoming much more widely available.

The recipes that follow are very lightly sweetened. Too much sugar masks the exuberant natural flavors of most fruits. Fruit ripened to its perfection needs very little adornment, so the recipes that follow are simple to prepare. You may wish to increase the sugar if the fruit you are using is a little underripe. Honey could be substituted in many of these recipes (except sorbets).

Most of the recipes that follow have reduced amounts of fat; some are very low in fat. Great taste has always been my top priority; reducing fat a close second.

For the most part I tend to bake with butter. One thing we do not consider in the whole low-fat issue is the *quality* of fats we use in our baking and cooking and the relationship of heart disease to trans fats or hydrogenated fats. I buy only cold-processed vegetable oils, butter, and olive oil—no hydrogenated fats. Some margarines sold at natural-foods stores, however, have very little additives and use only partially hydrogenated oils.

Many of these recipes can be made on the grill. After cooking the foods for a main course, I then arrange the grill for indirect heat, close the lid, and bake the dessert while enjoying dinner. (See chapter 2 for directions on indirect heat.)

Sorbets and Other Chilled Desserts

Sorbets are full of nutritious summer fruits (or vegetables) and are absolutely nonfat. An elegant finale to a meal, they are easy to prepare even if you don't own an ice cream or sorbet maker.

Sorbets should be light in texture and intense in flavor. They require just the right sugar content in order to freeze properly. Too much and the sorbet will remain wet and syrupy; too little and the liquids will form large ice crystals, giving a grainy texture. Sorbets do not keep well in the freezer like ice cream does. They are better if eaten within a few weeks.

To attain a smoother flavor and texture, I like to begin the sorbet preparation with a sugar syrup, especially if I don't use an ice cream maker. The syrup can be made quickly and this amount is sufficient for at least two recipes. (This may be cut in half if you feel you wouldn't use it frequently.) When cooled, the syrup can be refrigerated in a covered glass or plastic container for up to two weeks.

Sugar Syrup

Most grocery stores carry superfine sugar. It usually comes in one-pound boxes. Ask your grocer if you can't find it.

2 pounds superfine sugar   4 cups water

In a large saucepan, bring sugar and water to a gentle boil. Reduce heat until bubbles break the surface. Simmer 8 to 10 minutes. Remove from heat; cool before using or storing.

Strawberry Sorbet

4 cups fresh ripe strawberries
hulled and washed
2 cups Sugar Syrup (page 218)
Juice of ½ orange
or I heaping tablespoon
orange juice concentrate

Juice of ½ lemon
Garnish: Whole strawberries,
mint leaves, or edible flowers
(optional)

1. In a food processor or blender, process strawberries and 1 cup of the sugar syrup to a smooth puree. Add the remaining syrup, and orange and lemon juices. Pour into two 1-quart plastic or glass containers with tight lids. (I like to use old yogurt containers.)
2. Place in the freezer; freeze to a slush (1 to 2 hours). Return to the food processor/blender. Process until light and smooth.
3. Return to containers and freeze until firm. (This last step ensures a finer-textured sorbet, but I often forget to do it and the sorbet turns out fine.)
4. Garnish with a strawberry, mint leaf, or edible flower, if desired.

MAKES 2 QUARTS.

Variation: Substitute 4 cups pitted ripe apricots for the strawberries.

Chocolate Custard
with Fresh Raspberry Sauce and Cream

Small portions of this delectable dessert keep it light and make a perfect finale to a memorable meal. Containing no butter or eggs, it may require as long as 5 hours in the refrigerator to set.

5 ounces semisweet chocolate	½ cup sugar, divided
1½ cups skim milk	1 tablespoon cornstarch
(reserve ¼ cup)	1½ cups fresh raspberries
2 teaspoons instant coffee,	¼ cup sugar
preferably freeze-dried	Whipped cream
crystals	or Honey Yogurt Sauce
2 teaspoons rum	(page 158)
1 teaspoon vanilla extract	Garnish: Fresh raspberries

1. Break or cut the chocolate pieces into small chunks and place in a blender. Process a couple of times to break it up into still smaller pieces. Leave chocolate in the blender for later.
2. Pour 1¼ cups of the milk, instant coffee, rum, vanilla, and ¼ cup sugar into a medium-size saucepan. Add the cornstarch to the remaining ¼ cup of milk. Using medium-low heat and stirring continuously, slowly add the cornstarch and milk to the mixture. Bring the milk to a boil, continuing to stir so as not to allow the milk to scorch. Simmer gently for 2 to 3 minutes.
3. When the milk has finished cooking, pour it into the blender with the chocolate, cover, and let stand about 1 minute. Process until the mixture becomes smooth.

4. Pour the chocolate custard into a deep-dish pie pan or some other shallow pan. Refrigerate until set.
5. To prepare raspberry sauce, combine the raspberries and remaining ¼ cup sugar in a small saucepan (reserve 6 berries for garnish). Mash berries with a potato masher and simmer until sauce is warmed and slightly thickened. Serve chocolate custard in a small bowl and spoon the raspberry sauce over it. Top with a dollop of whipped cream or Honey Yogurt Sauce; garnish with a fresh raspberry.

MAKES 6 SERVINGS.

Raspberry Fool
with Mixed Berries

A fool is a frothy mixture of fruit and cream (in this definition). This is a somewhat lightened version because it uses nonfat yogurt in combination with whipping cream. It can be made with any summer fruit you have, but berries are best.

2 baskets (½ pint or 6 ounces) of raspberries
1½ cups whipping cream
2 cups nonfat yogurt
¼ cup sugar
2 tablespoons orange liqueur or orange juice concentrate

1½ cups mixed berries: blackberries, strawberries, blueberries; nectarine is great too

1. Mash raspberries with a potato masher and set aside. You may wish to press raspberries through cheesecloth to remove seeds (optional).
2. Whip the cream until fluffy, then fold in the yogurt. Fold in the raspberries and then the sugar and orange liqueur.
3. Top each serving with a generous amount of mixed berries.

MAKES 8 TO 10 SERVINGS.

Frozen Peach Yogurt

Frozen yogurt is a summer pleasure not to be missed. This recipe requires you to plan ahead to freeze the peaches, but then it is assembled just before serving and takes only minutes. Make it in the morning and surprise your family with this simple, nutritious dessert for dinner; or freeze the mixture in popsicle form and enjoy healthy fresh fruit treats. Place the frozen yogurt in the refrigerator just before you sit down for dinner or at least 20 minutes before serving.

I pound (about 4 medium-size) peaches (strawberries or a mix of berries also works well)	⅓ cup sugar
	I banana
	¾ cup low-fat yogurt
	I tablespoon lemon juice

1. Wash and remove seeds from the peaches; in a plastic bag, freeze peaches until solid. Peel and freeze one banana.
2. In a food processor or blender, combine frozen peaches with sugar, banana, yogurt, and lemon juice. Process until smooth.
3. Serve immediately or transfer to plastic container and freeze for up to one week. (Unlike ice cream, the quality of frozen yogurt diminishes in the freezer, so it is best kept for no more than a week.)

MAKES 3 CUPS, OR ABOUT 6 TO 8 SERVINGS.

Blackberry Soup
with Peaches

At the next barbecue, surprise your friends or family with this luscious fruit soup for dessert.

1½ pints blackberries, picked
over (about 4½ cups)
½ cup water
6 tablespoons sugar (or more)
1 teaspoon kirsch or brandy,
or 1 tablespoon orange juice
concentrate

3 large ripe peaches
(about 1½ pounds)
1 pint vanilla ice cream
or frozen yogurt

1. Rinse blackberries and remove any pieces of stems. Set aside 1 cup of berries.
2. Place the remaining 3½ cups of berries and ½ cup of water in a nonreactive medium-size saucepan. Cover, bring to a simmer over moderate heat, and cook until the berries have softened slightly, about 4 to 5 minutes.
3. Transfer the cooked berries to a strainer and press through to remove the seeds. Stir in 3 tablespoons sugar until dissolved; sweeten with more sugar if desired. Add the kirsch or orange juice. Refrigerate for one hour.
4. Just before serving, peel, halve, and pit the peaches. Working over a bowl, cut peaches into evenly shaped bite-size pieces. Sprinkle the remaining sugar over the peaches and toss gently.
5. Ladle the chilled blackberry soup into 6 soup bowls, add a scoop of ice cream, arrange the peach slices and 4 or 5 of the reserved blackberries around the edges. Serve immediately.

MAKES 6 SERVINGS.

Baked Desserts

Blue-Ribbon Blueberry Coffee Cake

This scrumptious cake could be used as a dessert or a breakfast cake. The recipe won a blue ribbon at the local county fair. I adjusted it to lower the fat but it's still very moist.

2½ cups all-purpose flour
   or whole-wheat pastry flour
1 teaspoon baking powder
¾ teaspoon baking soda
¾ cup butter at room
   temperature
1¼ cups sugar
1 teaspoon vanilla extract
¼ cup applesauce

½ teaspoon grated lemon rind
3 egg whites
1 cup low-fat yogurt

For blueberry filling and topping:
3 to 4 tablespoons sugar
1½ cups blueberries
½ cup chopped walnuts
1 teaspoon cinnamon

1. Mix together flour, baking powder, and soda. Set aside. In a large mixing bowl, add the butter, 1¼ cups sugar, vanilla, applesauce, and lemon rind. With a hand mixer, beat in egg whites one at a time, then the yogurt. At low speed, gradually beat in flour mixture until blended.

2. For the blueberry filling, stir together 2 tablespoons sugar, blueberries, and walnuts (chopped medium-fine).

3. Turn about one-third of the batter into a greased and floured 9-inch tube pan. Sprinkle with half the blueberry filling. Repeat layers. Spread with remaining batter.

4. For the topping, stir together 1 or 2 tablespoons sugar and the cinnamon. Sprinkle over batter.

5. Bake on the rack below center in a preheated 350-degree oven until a knife comes out free of batter—about 50 minutes. Cool completely. Loosen edges and around tube. Invert on a cake platter.

MAKES 8 TO 10 SERVINGS.

Almond Peaches
with Toasted Oat Shortcakes

1¼ cups rolled oats
    Vegetable oil or nonstick
    vegetable cooking spray
1 cup whole-wheat pastry
    flour or all-purpose flour
¼ cup sugar
2 teaspoons baking powder
1 teaspoon baking soda
½ teaspoon salt
¼ cup reduced-fat cream
    cheese

¾ cup buttermilk
1 tablespoon vegetable oil
1 teaspoon pure vanilla extract
6 to 7 peaches or nectarines
1 tablespoon butter
¼ cup honey
3 tablespoons lemon juice
1 tablespoon almond extract
1 pint vanilla frozen yogurt
    or Honey Yogurt Sauce
    (page 158)

1. Preheat oven to 350 degrees.
2. Spread oats on a small baking sheet or cake pan. Toast for 10 to 15 minutes, or until light golden and fragrant, stirring twice. Remove oats to a bowl. Increase oven temperature to 425 degrees. Lightly oil the baking sheet or coat it with nonstick vegetable spray.
3. In a mixing bowl, whisk together 1 cup of the oats, flour, sugar, baking powder, baking soda, and salt. Cut cream cheese into dry ingredients until mixture resembles coarse meal.
4. In a glass measuring cup, combine buttermilk, oil, and vanilla. Make a well in the dry ingredients. Add the wet ingredients and stir with a fork until just combined. (Dough will be wet and sticky; do not overmix.) Spoon dough into 8 mounds on prepared baking sheet. Sprinkle with remaining ¼ cup toasted oats. Bake shortcakes for 10 to 12 minutes, or until golden. Cool slightly before serving.

5. While shortcakes are baking, wash peaches and cut them into ½-inch cubes. In a medium-size saucepan, melt butter. Add the honey, lemon juice, and almond extract and heat through to blend. Add the cut-up peaches. Heat to warm through and coat peaches with the almond sauce.
6. To serve, split the shortcakes in half with a serrated knife. Spoon peach filling over the bottom half of shortcake and cover with the top half. Top with frozen yogurt or Honey Yogurt Sauce (page 158), if desired.

MAKES 8 SERVINGS.

Desserts on the Grill

Under certain conditions, baking on the grill works mar-velously. Success depends on the kind of grill you have. A minimum of two burners on a gas grill is essential. A kettle grill must be at least 21 to 24 inches in diameter to provide enough room. Preparing a grill for indirect heat is described in chapter 2 (page 11).

Baking on the grill is not quite the same as putting some-thing in the oven and trusting that it will come out perfect. You must know your grill. Most have hot spots. I often reopen the grill and turn a pan when it is half-cooked. Timing is also different for each situation, as grills vary. (Some grills have a temperature gauge on the outside.) Touch. Look. Use your own sense of what feels right.

Honey-Glazed Nectarines with Raspberries and Honey Yogurt Sauce

2 (½-pint) baskets of raspberries
⅓ to ½ cup sugar
4 medium-size nectarines
1 tablespoon melted butter
1 tablespoon lemon juice

Generous tablespoon
of honey
Honey Yogurt Sauce
(page 158) or a dollop
of vanilla yogurt

1. Light a fire in a grill or preheat a gas grill to medium-high.
2. In a blender or food processor, puree the raspberries and ⅓ cup sugar. If you choose to, force the puree through a sieve to remove the seeds. Refrigerate the raspberry puree until cold.
3. Halve and pit the nectarines. In a small saucepan, melt together the butter, lemon juice, and honey. Brush evenly over the nectarines, covering all sides. When the fire is hot, lay the nectarine halves on the rack, cut sides down. Grill, turning once, until they have light grill marks and are just heated through, about 3 to 5 minutes.
4. Place each nectarine on a small dessert plate. Spoon the raspberry sauce into the seed cavity of the nectarine and drizzle the Honey Yogurt Sauce over it all.

MAKES 8 SERVINGS.

Rhubarb Crisp

Rhubarb is less stringy if it is peeled before slicing. It's an easy task if you slip a small paring knife under the outer layer and pull off as much as possible.

¼ cup quick-cooking rolled oats
½ cup whole-wheat pastry
   flour or all-purpose white
   flour, divided
¼ cup powdered nonfat milk
¼ cup packed dark brown sugar
1¼ teaspoons cinnamon
2 tablespoons butter
   or margarine

¼ cup finely chopped nuts
   (optional)
5 cups (about 1½ pounds)
   rhubarb, peeled and cut into
   ½-inch slices
¼ cup orange juice
2 egg whites or 1 egg,
   lightly beaten
¾ cups sugar

1. Preheat a gas grill to medium or build a fire in a kettle grill and prepare coals for indirect heat as described in chapter 2 (page 11).
2. To prepare the topping, in a medium-size bowl combine the oats, ¼ cup flour, powdered milk, brown sugar, and cinnamon. Stir to mix the ingredients thoroughly. With a pastry blender or two knives, cut in the butter until the mixture looks like coarse meal. Then stir in the chopped nuts (optional).
3. To make the filling, combine the rhubarb, orange juice, and beaten egg whites or whole egg. Stir in the sugar and remaining ¼ cup flour. Pour the mixture into a 9-inch deep-dish pie plate. Sprinkle the flour mixture evenly over the surface of the fruit.

4. Bake the crisp for 35 to 40 minutes on a closed grill. Turn pan once if using a grill. This can also be baked in a 350-degree oven for 30 to 35 minutes.

SERVES 6 TO 8.

Variation: This is also great if 1 cup of sliced strawberries is substituted for 1 cup of the rhubarb.

Apricot Cherry Cobbler

Apricots have gone the way of tomatoes. Their delicate nature does not tolerate the abuse of mass transportation and national marketing, so varieties have been developed that are tough enough to stand up to mechanical handling and long-distance transportation. Alas, they have no flavor. At local fruit stands or farmers' markets, look for Blenheim apricots. They have a heady sweet-tart flavor and a velvety texture that melts on the tongue—the way apricots are supposed to taste.

Kirsch is a cherry-flavored liqueur. Some better-quality liquor stores carry it in small 2-ounce sample sizes, which are great for cooking.

1¾ cups whole-wheat pastry
flour
½ cup plus 2 tablespoons sugar,
divided
1 tablespoon baking powder
½ teaspoon salt
3 tablespoons butter
1 cup nonfat or low-fat milk
4 cups apricots, washed and
halved (about 15 to 18
medium-size ones)

1 to 1½ cups fresh cherries,
washed and pitted,
or 1 16-ounce can pitted
red pie cherries
⅓ cup cherry or orange juice
2 teaspoons kirsch (optional)
2 tablespoons cornstarch

1. Prepare the grill for indirect heat by following instructions in chapter 2 (page 11).
2. In a large bowl, sift together the flour, 2 tablespoons sugar, baking powder, and salt. Cut butter into dry ingredients; then make a well in the

center of the dough and pour in the milk. Stir until the dough is fairly free from the side of the bowl. Turn the dough onto a lightly floured board. Knead gently and quickly. Roll with a lightly floured rolling pin until the dough is ½-inch thick. Cut to the shape of the baking pan you are using.

3. Combine remaining ½ cup sugar with the apricots and cherries. Place them in a 6-by-9-inch baking dish. (Disposable aluminum foil pans are sometimes useful on the grill.)

4. In a small bowl, combine the cherry juice and kirsch. Stir in the cornstarch and pour over fruit. Lay the cobbler dough over the entire pan, patching where necessary.

5. Bake on the grill for 35 to 50 minutes, depending on how hot it is; or bake in a 350-degree oven for 30 to 40 minutes.

MAKES 6 TO 8 SERVINGS.

Blueberry Peach Cobbler on the Grill

This cobbler from the grill is a highlight of the summer and always gets recipe requests.

½ cup plus 1 tablespoon butter, divided
1¼ cups whole-wheat pastry flour or a mixture of white and wheat flours
1 tablespoon baking powder
¼ teaspoon salt
½ cup sugar
¾ cup milk

4 cups washed, sliced peaches
1½ cups fresh or frozen blueberries
¼ to ⅓ cup sugar or 2 tablespoons honey (depending on sweetness of fruit)
2 to 3 tablespoons lemon juice
1 tablespoon almond extract

1. When coals in a kettle grill have cooled to a medium temperature, prepare for indirect heat; or preheat a gas grill for indirect heat following instructions in chapter 2 (page 11).
2. In a small saucepan, melt ½ cup butter.
3. Measure and add together the flour, baking powder, salt, and ½ cup sugar in a large bowl. Add the milk and melted butter and stir to combine. Set aside.
4. Combine the peaches and blueberries in a 6-by-9-inch baking pan.
5. Using the same saucepan, melt the remaining tablespoon of butter and add ¼ to ⅓ cup sugar or 2 tablespoons honey, lemon juice, and almond extract just to warm through. Pour this mixture over the blueberries and peaches; mix to combine.

6. Spread the cobbler dough evenly over the fruit. Cover tightly with aluminum foil. Bake to a golden brown over medium heat on the grill—about 35 to 50 minutes. Remove foil the last 20 minutes of baking.

MAKES 8 TO 10 SERVINGS.

Variation: Top this cobbler with Frozen Peach Yogurt (page 223) for a double peach flavor.

Peach Upside-Down Cake
on the Grill

This cake is light and delicious. A cast-iron skillet works well on the grill. It's best to turn the pan once or twice so that it will heat evenly.

5 tablespoons butter, divided
½ cup brown sugar
1 tablespoon orange juice concentrate or Grand Marnier
5 large peaches (or equivalent amount of pears, pineapple, or plums)

1 cup whole-wheat pastry flour
1¼ teaspoons baking powder
¼ teaspoon salt
1 egg plus 2 egg whites
½ cup sugar

1. Prepare a grill for indirect heat by following instructions in chapter 2 (page 11).
2. In a 9- or 10-inch ovenproof skillet, melt 4 tablespoons of the butter. Add the brown sugar and orange juice concentrate; stir, cooking until the sugar has dissolved to form a syrup. Remove and set aside.
3. Thickly slice the peaches and pack them tightly across the melted butter-sugar mixture in the skillet. Set aside.
4. In a medium-size bowl, add the flour, baking powder, and salt. Set aside.
5. Separate the eggs, breaking the whites into a large bowl and one yolk into a small bowl. Melt the remaining tablespoon of butter in a small skillet. Add the butter and orange juice concentrate to the egg yolk. Whisk to combine.

6. Beat the egg whites with an electric beater or a whisk until they form firm peaks. Do not overbeat. Fold the sugar into the egg whites about ¼ cup at a time. Fold in the egg yolk mixture. Fold in the flour mixture.
7. Pour the batter over the peaches and spread with a spatula to cover. Bake on the grill until a toothpick inserted into the center comes out clean—about 25 to 30 minutes. Remove and let stand at least 10 minutes before unmolding.
8. To unmold, run a knife around the edges of the cake, then place a large plate over the top of the skillet. Hold the plate and the skillet tightly together and flip them over so that the skillet is on top. The cake will fall onto the plate. Serve warm.

MAKES 6 TO 8 SERVINGS.

Note: Many liquor stores carry 2-ounce sample bottles that are great for cooking.

Ginger Pear Crumble

This simple dessert is just enough to satisfy. Try adding a small amount of ginger (powder) to the whipped cream as well.

¾ cup whole-wheat pastry
  flour or all-purpose
  white flour
1 tablespoon grated lemon
  zest
⅔ cup brown sugar

¼ cup butter
5 cups sliced pears
1 tablespoon lemon juice
1 tablespoon fresh grated ginger
  Dollop of whipped cream or
  frozen yogurt

1. Prepare grill for indirect heat as described in chapter 2 (page 11).
2. Mix the flour, lemon zest, and brown sugar in a bowl. Using a pastry cutter, two knives, or a food processor, cut the butter into the flour mixture until texture is crumbly but not sticky.
3. Place the pear slices in an 8-by-8-inch square baking dish, spreading them evenly. Sprinkle with lemon juice and grated ginger. Spoon the crumb mixture over the pears.
4. Bake on the grill for 20 to 30 minutes, checking for doneness periodically (when the pears are tender and the top is browned). This dish will be juicy.
5. Serve straight from the grill with a dollop of whipped cream or frozen yogurt.

MAKES 6 TO 8 SERVINGS.

Variation: Substitute 5 cups of sliced plums for the pears and 1 teaspoon cinnamon for the ginger.

Gratin of Pears and Fennel

4 pears	¼ cup whole-wheat pastry
4 tablespoons sugar, divided	flour or all-purpose flour
3 tablespoons melted butter	Pinch of salt
I egg	I to I½ teaspoons fennel
¼ cup milk	¼ cup chopped almonds

1. Peel, core, and quarter the pears. Sprinkle 1 tablespoon of the sugar and 1 tablespoon of the melted butter in the bottom of a shallow 9-inch baking dish. Place pears in this dish.

2. In a small bowl, whisk together the egg, milk, and remaining 2 tablespoons of butter. Add the flour and salt to make a batter. In a blender or food processor, process the fennel seeds until they are finely ground. Add the fennel to the batter and spoon this batter over the pears.

3. In the same blender, finely chop the almonds. Add the remaining 3 tablespoons of sugar to the almonds and sprinkle over the top of the batter. Cover dish with aluminum foil and place on medium heat on the grill for 15 to 20 minutes or until top is crisp and pears are softened. (Remove the aluminum foil the last 10 minutes of cooking.)

MAKES 4 TO 6 SERVINGS.

Kristin's Grilled Apple Cake

The new crop of apples is one of the first signs of fall. This apple cake captures the essence of summer's sweetness. Make it on the grill or in the oven. It is a specialty of my friend, Kristin Liljequist.

½ cup butter or margarine
1½ cups sugar
1 egg plus 1 egg white
2 tablespoons low-fat milk
1 teaspoon vanilla extract
2 cups whole-wheat pastry
  flour or all-purpose flour
1 teaspoon salt
1 teaspoon baking soda

1 tablespoon cinnamon
1 teaspoon nutmeg
4 cups chopped apples
  (peeling optional)
1 cup raisins
1 cup chopped nuts
Honey Yogurt Sauce
(page 158) or ice cream

1. If using an oven, preheat to 375 degrees. Otherwise, build a fire in a kettle grill and prepare for indirect heat or preheat one burner of a gas grill to medium-high.

2. In a bowl, cream together the butter and sugar. Add the eggs, milk, and vanilla and continue to beat with an electric mixer.

3. In a separate bowl, measure and add the flour, salt, soda, cinnamon, nutmeg, apples, raisins, and nuts. Mix lightly. Add the wet ingredients to this bowl and stir well with a spoon.

4. To bake in an oven, pour mixture into a 9-by-13-inch baking dish and bake for 1 hour at 375 degrees.

5. To cook on a grill, pour cake mixture into a well-greased 12-inch cast-iron skillet that has been sprinkled with a small amount of flour. Cover

with aluminum foil and roast (with lid of grill down) 40 to 50 minutes. Check and turn the pan so that it heats evenly. Remove foil after 30 minutes of cooking. Serve with Honey Yogurt Sauce (page 158) or ice cream.

MAKES 8 TO 12 SERVINGS.

Blueberry Pear Crisp

¾ cups firmly packed brown
sugar
½ cup whole-wheat pastry
flour or all-purpose flour
¾ cups rolled oats
1 teaspoon cinnamon
3 tablespoons butter
or margarine (at room
temperature)
1 tablespoon low-fat milk

½ cup chopped walnuts
(optional)
3 to 4 ripe pears or apples
1¼ cups fresh or frozen
blueberries
2 tablespoons lemon
or apple juice
1 teaspoon grated lemon zest
(optional)
Ice cream or Honey Yogurt
Sauce (page 158)

1. Adjust coals in a kettle grill for indirect heat or preheat one burner of a gas grill to medium. If using an oven, preheat to 350 degrees.
2. In a medium-size bowl, stir together the sugar, flour, oats, and cinnamon. Cut in butter until mixture is crumbly; mix in milk. Add chopped walnuts and set aside.
3. Cut pears into bite-size pieces. Place blueberries and pears in a square aluminum foil baking dish or a metal cake pan used for the grill. Sprinkle with juice and lemon peel. Toss to coat fruit. Sprinkle the crumb mixture evenly over the fruit.
4. If using an oven, bake for 30 to 40 minutes. If cooking over the grill, cover the pan with aluminum foil and bake at medium temperature, turning the pan once to ensure even heat—about 25 to 35 minutes or until pears are fork-tender and topping is crisp. Remove the foil the last 15 minutes of baking. Serve warm with ice cream or Honey Yogurt Sauce (page 158).

MAKES 6 SERVINGS.

S'Mores

The grilling season ends. The rains (or snow) come and we are indoors. Our culinary time clock is yearning for pumpkin pie, Christmas cookies, and hearty soups by the fire (accompanied by a video).

The last recipe in this book is one that can't be missed. Though not particularly healthy, it guarantees to nourish the child in all of us. It is best cooked over a real fire and accompanied by the singing of friends.

I square of a plain chocolate candy bar	2 graham cracker squares
	2 large marshmallows

1. Prepare a medium-hot fire or use an existing fire that has burned down.
2. Place chocolate on top of one graham cracker square.
3. Thread 1 or 2 marshmallows on a stick or long metal skewer and toast directly over glowing coals, turning every few seconds, until cooked to perfection.
4. Quickly slide marshmallows onto the graham cracker and chocolate. Gently press the second graham crackers on top so that the warmth of the marshmallows will melt the chocolate. Eat immediately.

MAKES I SERVING. (TWO PER PERSON SHOULD BE MORE THAN S'NOUGH.)

Suggested Menus
for Memorable Meals

EXCITING CONTRASTS MAKE A MEMORABLE MEAL. TASTE, COLOR, and texture come together to form a balance. Of course, good friends and good conversation are important ingredients, but that's another book.

Creating a menu from the grill takes different planning than when cooking on the stove. Foods come off the grill fast and are ready to eat, so having the other dishes prepared ahead of time becomes essential. Many of the vegetable and salad dishes in this book are served at room temperature. They can be ready before the final round of last-minute foods to be grilled. The oven can also be used to hold food at a warm temperature until you're ready to serve.

Many of the desserts in this book are easy to prepare before guests arrive. Put them on the grill just as you are ready to sit down for dinner. Your guests will be finishing the last morsels as the scent of dessert begins to float off the grill. Other desserts are best cooked ahead of time and then returned to the grill to rewarm prior to serving.

If you're working with a kettle grill, remember the foods that need to be cooked at the highest temperature should be cooked first. If you plan to bake or roast foods using indirect heat, they should be cooked after that.

When the grill is hot for a simple weeknight dinner, I often grill small amounts of foods that I might use for another day, such as roasted garlic, tomatoes, or peppers. The more I experiment, the more I find that my favorite dishes are even more delectable when grilled.

Enjoy and be well!

MENUS FOR A FULL MEAL
OR ENTERTAINING

✻

Grilled Artichokes with Cilantro Pesto (page 109)

salad of mixed greens

Fusilli with Grilled Asparagus and Canellini Beans (page 44)

Strawberry Sorbet (page 219)

✻

Grilled Portobello Mushroom and Asparagus Salad (page 212)

Roasted Garlic and Red Pepper Soup (page 187)

Charcoal-Grilled Leeks (page 117)

Focaccia (page 98) or other crusty bread

Rhubarb Crisp (page 232)

✻

Grilled Vegetable Paella (page 57)

Cucumber, Avocado, and Red Pepper Salsa (page 167)

Garlic Breadsticks (page 100)

✻

salad of mixed greens

Grilled Polenta and Peppers with Fontina Cheese (page 26)

Grilled Eggplant with Basil Pesto (pages 114 and 152)

Chocolate Custard with Fresh Raspberry Sauce and Cream (page 220)

✻

Gazpacho Rose (page 177)

Warm Spinach and Basil Salad (page 200)

Jim and Renee's Potato Packets Especialle (page 48)

Peach Upside-Down Cake on the Grill (page 238)

✳

Light and Easy Zucchini Soup (page 182)

Summer Vegetable Kabobs with Seitan (page 122)

Sautéed Couscous with Pine Nuts and Garlic (page 53)

Blueberry Peach Cobbler on the Grill (page 236)

✳

Marinated and Grilled Summer Squash (page 120)

Nut Burgers (page 61)

Roasted Potato Wedges (page 75)

Kristin's Grilled Apple Cake (page 242)

✳

Gazpacho (page 176)

or Kamp Bell's Creamy Tomato Soup (page 183)

Grilled Polenta with Mushrooms (page 30)

Grilled Vegetable Ratatouille (page 128)

bread

Ginger Pear Crumble (page 240)

✳

Mediterranean Shepherd's Soup (page 184)

Roasted Herbs and Vegetables (page 134)

Focaccia on the Grill (page 98)

or other crusty bread

Gratin of Pears and Fennel (page 241)

✳

SIMPLE SUMMER SUPPERS

✳

Corn-Stuffed Bell Peppers (page 138)

Black Bean Salsa (page 165)

warm tortillas or quesadillas

✳

Grilled Tomatoes with Red Onions and Basil (page 119)

Basil Beer Bread (page 97)

✳

Gazpacho (page 176)

Garlic and Arugula Pizza (page 94)

✳

Warm Spinach and Basil Salad (page 200)

Tomato Bruschetta (page 85)

✳

Ragout of Summer Vegetables with Tarragon (page 125)

Potatoes Alfredo (page 50)

✳

Mexican Pizzas on the Grill (page 95)

Grilled Corn and Avocado Salsa (page 166)

✳

Bulgur and Beans (page 52)

Roasted Corn with Cilantro Butter (page 112)

✳

Teriyaki Tofu Steaks (page 66)

Chinese Chicken-less Salad (page 195)

✳

Make Your Own Pizzas (page 88)

Roasted Red Pepper Dip (page 163)

raw or grilled vegetables (pages 106-107)

✳

Index

Custard, Chocolate, with Fresh
Raspberry Sauce and Cream,
220–221

D

Desserts, 216–245
Almond Peaches with Toasted Oat
Shortcakes, 228–229
Apricot Cherry Cobbler, 234–235
Baked, 226–229
Berry Soup with a Sparkle, 179
Blackberry Soup with Peaches,
224
Blueberry Peach Cobbler on the
Grill, 236–237
Blueberry Pear Crisp, 244
Blue-Ribbon Blueberry Coffee
Cake, 226–227
Chilled, 217–224
Chocolate Custard with Fresh
Raspberry Sauce and Cream,
220–221
Frozen Peach Yogurt, 223
Ginger Pear Crumble, 240
Gratin of Pears and Fennel, 241
Grilled, 238–245
Honey-Glazed Nectarines with
Raspberries and Honey Yogurt
Sauce, 231
Kristin's Grilled Apple Cake,
242–243
Peach Upside-Down Cake on the
Grill, 238–239

Desserts *cont.*
Raspberry Fool with Mixed
Berries, 222
Rhubarb Crisp, 232–233
S'Mores, 245
Strawberry Sorbet, 219
Sugar Syrup, 218
Dill Pickles, Easy Refrigerator, 171
Dip(s). *See also* Spread(s)
Roasted Red Pepper, 163

E

Eggplant
Caponata, 196–197
Roasted Red, White, and Blue
Black Casserole, 132–133
Slices, Grilled, 114
and Tomato Gratin, Roasted, 115
Eileen's Salad Dressing or Marinade,
148

F

Fennel and Pears, Gratin of, 241
Fettuccine with Roasted Tomatoes
and Garlic, 41
Fire
preparing, 13–14
safety guidelines, 15
temperature of, 16–17
Focaccia on the Grill, 98–99
Franks and Beans, Barbecued, 70–71

Y

Yogurt
Dill Dressing, Green Bean Salad
with, 202
Frozen, Peach, 223
Honey Sauce, 158

Z

Zucchini. *See* Squash